Shawn's Fundamentals
of Dance

LANGUAGE OF DANCE SERIES

EDITOR

Ann Hutchinson Guest
Director of the Language of Dance Centre
London, UK

ASSOCIATE EDITOR

Ray Cook
Vassar College
Poughkeepsie, New York, USA

No. 1:
The Flower Festival in Genzano: Pas de Deux
Edited by Ann Hutchinson Guest

No. 2:
Shawn's Fundamentals of Dance
Edited by Ann Hutchinson Guest

Other volumes in preparation

Soirée Musicale
The First White Ballet
The Pas de Six from "La Vivandière"

ISSN 0888-1286

This book is part of a series. The publisher will accept continuation orders that may be cancelled at any time and that provide for automatic billing and shipping of each title in the series upon publication. Please write for details.

Shawn's Fundamentals of Dance

EDITED BY

Ann Hutchinson Guest

Director of the Language of Dance Centre
London

CHOREOGRAPHY BY

TED SHAWN

MUSIC BY

JESS MEEKER

Recorded in Labanotation by
ANN HUTCHINSON GUEST

GORDON AND BREACH
New York   London   Paris   Montreux   Tokyo   Melbourne

Gordon and Breach Science Publishers

Post Office Box 786
Cooper Station
New York, New York 10276
United States of America

Post Office Box 161
1820 Montreux 2
Switzerland

Post Office Box 197
London WC2E 9PX
England

3-14-9 Okubo
Shinjuku-ku, Tokyo
Japan

58, rue Lhomond
75005 Paris
France

Private Bag 8
Camberwell, Victoria 3124
Australia

Cover Photo:
Barton Mumaw performing the *pas de poisson*
jump described on pages 36 and 37.
Courtesy of the Dance Collection,
New York Public Library.

Library of Congress Cataloguing in Publication Data

Shawn's Fundamentals of Dance.
Shawn, Ted, 1891–1972.
    Fundamentals of preliminary dance training.

    (Language of dance series, ISSN 0888–1286 ; no. 2)
    Includes index.
    1. Dancing – Study and teaching.   2. Exercise.
I. Meeker, Jess.   II. Guest, Ann Hutchinson.
III. Title.   IV. Series.
GV1589.S52   1988   792.3'07   87–21091
ISBN 2–88124–219–7 (Switzerland)

TABLE OF CONTENTS

INTRODUCTION TO THE SERIES

The *Language of Dance* series aims to expand the literature of dance through publication of key works that cover a range of dance styles and dance periods.

Through careful selection of appropriate movement description, these gems of dance heritage have been translated into Labanotation, the highly developed method of analyzing and recording movement.

A language is spoken, written and read. Those intimately involved in the study and performance of dance will have experienced the language of dance in its "spoken" form, i.e. when it is danced. During the years spent in mastering a dance form, the component parts are discovered and become part of one's dance language. Through the written form of dance the building blocks common to all forms of dance become clear, as well as how these blocks are used. The study of the Language of Dance incorporates these basic elements and the way the various component parts are put together to produce choreographic sentences. How the movement sequences are performed, the manner of "uttering" them, rests on the individual interpretation.

In the *Language of Dance Series* understanding of the material is enriched through Study and Performance Notes which provide an aid in exploring the movement sequences and bringing them to life.

Ann Hutchinson Guest, Editor

ACKNOWLEDGEMENTS

Many people have contributed over the years to the preparation of this book. The idea first took shape during the summers I taught Labanotation at Jacob's Pillow when I also took part in as many classes as my own teaching allowed. I had already notated Shawn's *16 Dances in 16 Rhythms* and approached him with the possibility of recording some of his other works. These Fundamental Exercises seemed an obvious choice, primarily because of our shared concern with dance education. The revival of interest in Shawn's work and the need for teaching material of this kind have spurred the final preparation of *Shawn's Fundamentals of Dance.*

Jennifer Scanlon, later a leading dancer with the José Limón Company, spent the summer of 1956 at Jacob's Pillow as a scholarship student assigned to notating Shawn's classes. Barton Mumaw, the leading dancer with Shawn's Men's Group, who has long used this basic training material in his classes, has graciously and generously contributed valuable verbal instructions highlighting the salient points of each exercise as well as sharing his own teaching notes. I am much indebted to him for his enthusiasm and support. Jess Meeker, Shawn's original accompanist, unhesitatingly contributed his time and talent in answering music questions and in making the cassette tape to accompany the book.

Juli Nunlist's careful reading of the text assured that it would be comprehensible to the non-dancer. The Language of Dance Centre staff undertook details of production in many roles. Jane Whitear undertook the role of production assistant as well as the autography of the Labanotation which was proofread by Rob van Haarst. Nancy Harlock took part in checking and coordinating the text and index which were further refined through Jude Sidall's discerning comments. Cerinda Survant contributed additional revisions and improvements on the text and passed on her word processor expertise to Rob van Haarst who finalized the appearance of the text.

I am much endebted for all help given by Barton Mumaw, Jacob's Pillow and the Dance Collection of the New York Public Library in my search for photographs.

To conclude, I acknowledge with great appreciation the work of Ray Cook, my Associate Editor of this Language of Dance Series, who questioned every symbol and every word from both the dancer's and the dance notator's point of view.

To all the above I extend my heart-felt thanks.

TED SHAWN
wearing the Cross of Dannebrog.

SHAWN'S FOREWORD

Regardless of what type of dancing a pupil may ultimately choose, there are certain constants — abilities, skills — that everyone must master. We expect of every dancer that he have muscular strength, elasticity of the entire body, coordination of all parts of the body, ability to move musically and rhythmically, to have a rich vocabulary of movement, to have mastered spatial aspects both in regard to his own movement and in relation to a group of other dancers.

In contrast to all the other arts, the dancer has the additional task of having to develop his own body as his instrument and as the material of his art form. Therefore the first essential, before the dance as such is approached, is to develop and train the body until it becomes instantly and completely responsive to any command the brain gives.

Muscular strength must be built up through the right kinds of exercise to enable the dancer, for example, to leap into the air and to land without shock or jar. All stiffness must be eliminated, so that fluid movement may pass through all or any part of the body like a wave. The rhythmic and ever-present principle of tension and relaxation must be so much a part of the dancer that he or she can use energy or release energy at will, even in small space and time units. The dancer must understand and be able to produce many different qualities of movement, and develop the ability to improvise as readily as he or she engages in conversation.

No claim is made that the following exercises are complete, or that they produce the only *good* system; there are many. These are the net result of a study of worthwhile systems of physical training available today, plus the personal contributions I have made as a result of over twenty-five years of continuous teaching.

"By their fruit ye shall know them." The use of these exercises has borne much good fruit. I believe that all of the best teachers of dance in America today use all of these principles — and that they differ only in terminology and in the forms of application. But the infinite variety of forms in which a principle may be legitimately and profitably employed is one of the strongest fascinations of dance training. As soon as a principle of movement is thoroughly understood, anyone can apply that principle in forms of his own devising with equally good results. As for freshness of interest, teachers and pupils should constantly devise new forms in which to use these eternal principles. It is only hoped that the convenient form of these exercises, plus the music written by Jess Meeker, a composer who has studied and worked with the rhythms of bodily movement for many years, will be of benefit to those who have not as yet worked out original training routines.

As "pre-dance body training" nothing here presented pretends to have yet entered the realm of dance itself, nor are questions of the *art* of the dance itself even touched upon. The purpose of these exercises is specifically to get the student's body in such condition, and his mind-body coordination to such a state that, when he begins to learn a specific dance form or dance style, he will have an instrument that will respond almost unconsciously — a perfect and effortless instrument of his will.

Ted Shawn
Jacob's Pillow
1939

PREFACE

Dance techniques, especially contemporary ones, have developed significantly since Shawn wrote the above introduction in 1939. Kinesiology, bio-mechanics and other anatomically derived studies have contributed valuable knowledge to the training of a dancer. Improved knowledge of the body — the very instrument of dance — has produced remarkable techniques. However technically accomplished today's dancers are, we see they have a more limited expressive range than their predecessors; too often they are less able to convey the full scope of qualities of movement, and all too often exhibit an absence of cognitive understanding of their dance material. In short, they lack a balanced dance education. How is their training different from their predecessors, "the historical moderns"?

Shawn's Fundamentals of Dance provides a methodical yet organic approach to movement, a series of stepping stones that simultaneously develop physical and cognitive understanding of movement. The exercises vary greatly in movement quality; the student experiences these contrasts in his own body and soon perceives how other, more specialized dance techniques are created from materials as simple as these.

This book is especially valuable for the teacher who — even though highly skilled in one or another form of dance technique — seeks a different approach to the teaching of beginning students.

I met this material personally while a student of Shawn's at Jacob's Pillow. While my own technique was then somewhat more advanced than many of these exercises, I still found the material enjoyable and of value. I also observed its impact on the beginning students in the class. I have since drawn on it in many contexts, including working with adult amateurs.

Books on modern (contemporary) dance technique are rare: the necessary subtleties do not lend themselves to words and pictures: for this reason, text is provided to accompany the Labanotation. For those not yet fluent in notation, these word notes include images that embody the quality each particular exercise seeks to evoke in the student, images that focus the student's attention on the pertinent performance details.

Ann Hutchinson Guest
London

In this solo, *Invocation to the Thunderbird*, the contrast that Shawn has used in the oppositionally contracted and extended limbs achieved at the height of the vertical jump expresses inner power, determination, and a strong sense of dignity and presence.

INTRODUCTION

Shawn was concerned with the principles of movement and with formulating sequences through which these could be studied. These principles centered on body isolations and coordinations, spatial patterns, body weight, both in transference of weight in supporting and in use of weight (i.e. gravity) in gestures, and contrasts in use of energy (dynamics) and in movement durations (rhythms). While the physical and spatial "shape" of the movements and the "textures" used were important, Shawn did not emphasize precise performance, particularly not in exact placement of the limbs; students were allowed some leeway. Therefore the notation indicates the standard version, not the definitive one.

In many instances general timing has been given in the notation, general timing being the indication of the main beat on which the movement falls. However, exact timing is used when such precision affects the resulting quality of movement, the placement of emphasis and use of momentary pauses. As with dance in general, the performer should relate to the music and be affected by it.

SELECTION OF PHOTOGRAPHS

The following photographs have been included since they illustrate not only some of the movements in *Shawn's Fundamentals of Dance* but also his sense of movement line and use of space in the individual body as well as in group formations. Shawn used the fundamental movement principles as a basis for choreographic invention. Nowhere is this more appropriately illustrated than in his group work, *Kinetic Molpai*, created for his Men's Group and, decades later, successfully revived and performed to acclaim. The enjoyment of the young, contemporary performers in dancing these movements from an earlier period was clearly evident.

A demonstration of the THREE JUMPS by the Men's Group.
(See pages 42, 43.)

Barton Mumaw performing the split jump featured in the THREE JUMPS, taken from the group work
Kinetic Molpai.

In this Flamenco dance the circular path of the arm gestures are made more visible through use of the cloak. This solo, entitled "Hacendado de California," was from *O Libertad!*

Tension produced by the twists in the torso and arms combine with natural opposition of arms and legs in this American Indian solo, the *Osage-Pawnee Dance of Greeting*.

A defiance of gravity in a controlled descent combined with a clear monolinear body design. This study in balance is here performed in the costume of Shawn's solo *Frohsinn* (Spirit of Joy).

Relating to gravity through lowering with an expression of weight directed to the earth, the general body line made three-dimensional and hence more human through the torso twist. "Nobody Knows the Trouble I've Seen" from *Four American Dances*.

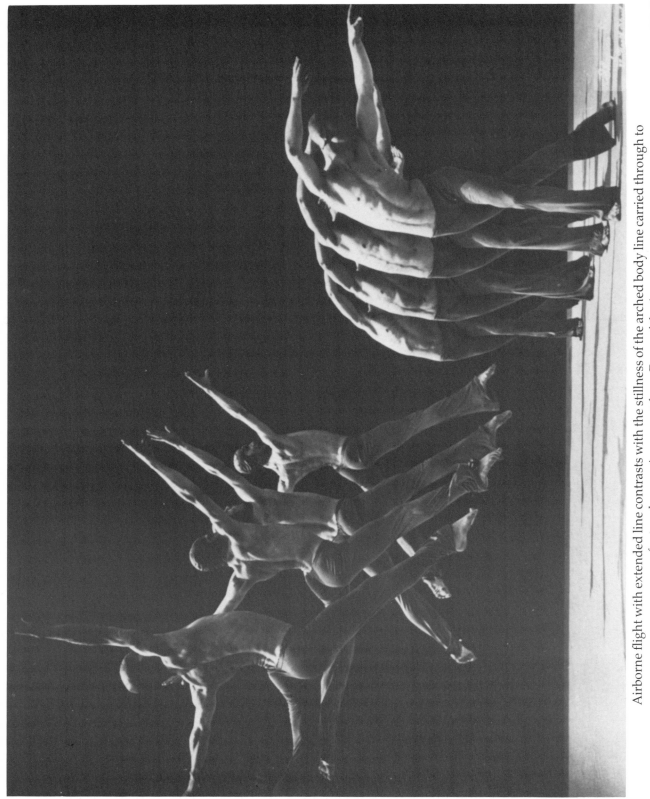

Airborne flight with extended line contrasts with the stillness of the arched body line carried through to foot and arms. A moment from *Dance of the Ages.*

Courtesy of the Dance Collection, New York Public Library.

The center figure, Shawn, illustrates the famous Denishawn pas de basque, a suspended curve from toes to hands in which the center of gravity is momentarily off balance. From *Kinetic Molpai.*

Courtesy of the Dance Collection, New York Public Library.

Clarity of line, variation in level, but unity in focus give strength to this simple group formation. From the Negro Spiritual *Go Down Moses.*

Courtesy of the Dance Collection, New York Public Library.

THE MUSIC SCORE

The printed music is coordinated with the dance through use of the same section marks, i.e. the "boxed" letters, A, B, C, etc. The measures are identically numbered in both the notation and the music. Numbers for repeated measures are indicated in parentheses.

THE MUSIC TAPE

Jess Meeker, Shawn's longtime accompanist and the composer of the music, has captured on tape the tempos and dynamics needed for each sequence.

On the music tape spoken identifications are given for each title, number and letter. Statement of meter and length of the introduction to each exercise are also included. In most sequences the letters are spoken over the continuously played music to aid location of the sections. For study purposes the General Stretching Set and Tension and Relaxation Set Two are recorded twice: first section by section, and then with continuously played music. For the Single Arm Swing and Development the music is repeated for the basic arm swing, but not for the repitition of the entire sequence to the other side.

The music for the Alphabet of Basic Steps is to be found in the music score but has not been included on the tape.

LABANOTATION GLOSSARY

The Labonotation is based on the standard description. In some instances the idea or concept of the movement, such as a circular path for a limb, joint or torso which may not be immediately evident from the sequence of symbols, is written alongside, placed in parentheses (curved vertical bows). Such additional clarification has not been given any time significance..

Timing is specific when the exact movement that an action occurs needs to be stressed or where it reveals more clearly the phrasing. General timing is used for simple sequences where the timing is obvious and need not be pin-pointed.

The rotational state of the legs is given for each exercise. When another exercise on the same page uses the same rotated state, the indication is not repeated.

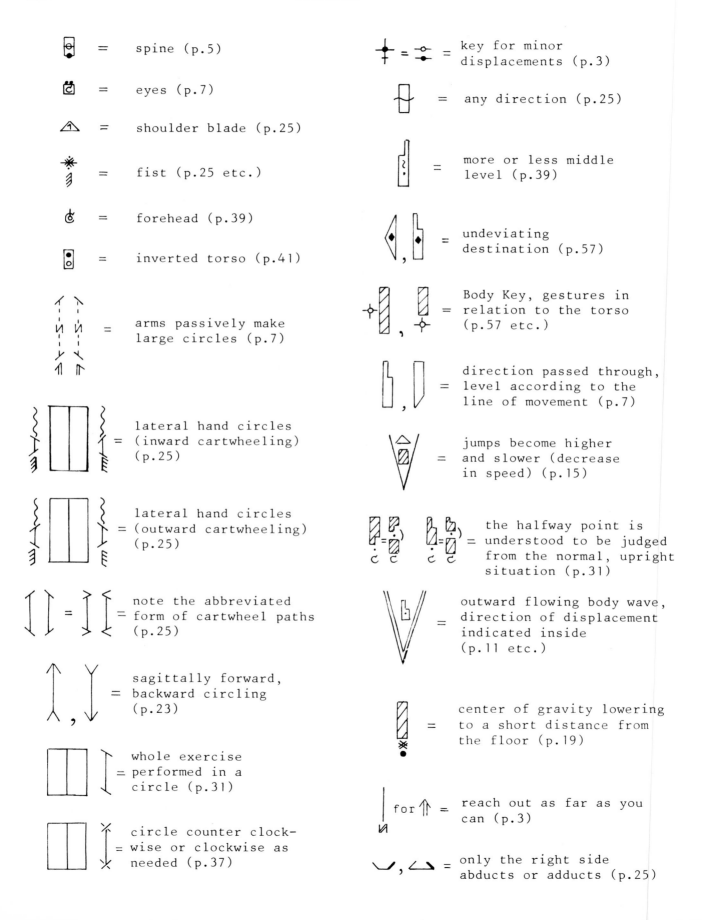

= spine (p.5)

= eyes (p.7)

= shoulder blade (p.25)

= fist (p.25 etc.)

= forehead (p.39)

= inverted torso (p.41)

= arms passively make large circles (p.7)

= lateral hand circles (inward cartwheeling) (p.25)

= lateral hand circles (outward cartwheeling) (p.25)

= note the abbreviated form of cartwheel paths (p.25)

= sagittally forward, backward circling (p.23)

= whole exercise performed in a circle (p.31)

= circle counter clockwise or clockwise as needed (p.37)

= key for minor displacements (p.3)

= any direction (p.25)

= more or less middle level (p.39)

= undeviating destination (p.57)

= Body Key, gestures in relation to the torso (p.57 etc.)

= direction passed through, level according to the line of movement (p.7)

= jumps become higher and slower (decrease in speed) (p.15)

= the halfway point is understood to be judged from the normal, upright situation (p.31)

= outward flowing body wave, direction of displacement indicated inside (p.11 etc.)

= center of gravity lowering to a short distance from the floor (p.19)

for = reach out as far as you can (p.3)

= only the right side abducts or adducts (p.25)

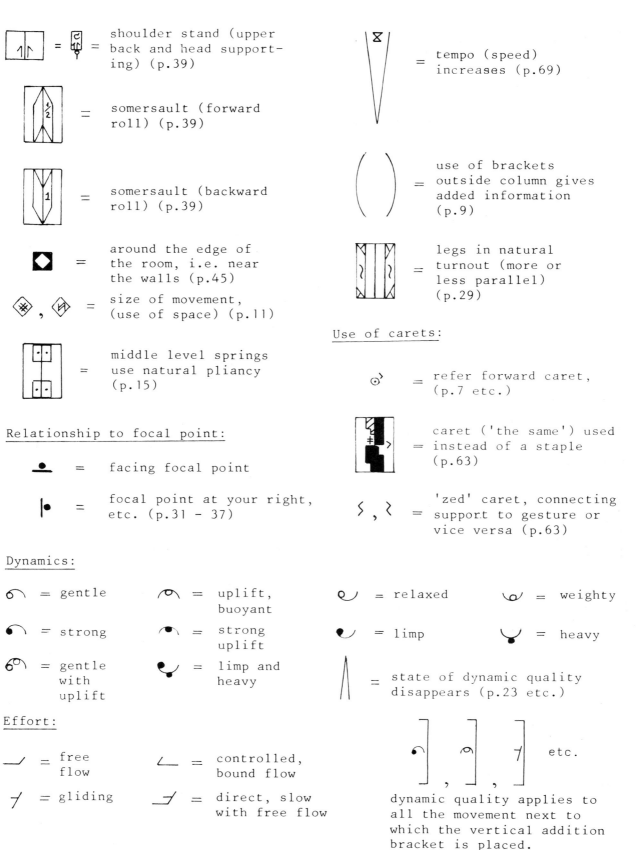

= shoulder stand (upper back and head supporting) (p.39)

= somersault (forward roll) (p.39)

= somersault (backward roll) (p.39)

= around the edge of the room, i.e. near the walls (p.45)

= size of movement, (use of space) (p.11)

= middle level springs use natural pliancy (p.15)

Relationship to focal point:

= facing focal point

= focal point at your right, etc. (p.31 - 37)

Dynamics:

= gentle   = uplift, buoyant   = relaxed   = weighty

= strong   = strong uplift   = limp   = heavy

= gentle with uplift   = limp and heavy

Effort:

= free flow   = controlled, bound flow

= gliding   = direct, slow with free flow

= tempo (speed) increases (p.69)

= use of brackets outside column gives added information (p.9)

= legs in natural turnout (more or less parallel) (p.29)

Use of carets:

= refer forward caret, (p.7 etc.)

= caret ('the same') used instead of a staple (p.63)

= 'zed' caret, connecting support to gesture or vice versa (p.63)

= state of dynamic quality disappears (p.23 etc.)

etc.

dynamic quality applies to all the movement next to which the vertical addition bracket is placed.

Ted Shawn teaching at Jacob's Pillow,
Jess Meeker at the piano.

STUDY AND PERFORMANCE NOTES

The following system of exercises is for use in preliminary dance training. The word notes are given in some detail since these segments are important studies in many kinds of movement, any one of which can be developed as improvisation, or as themes for dance studies. In teaching beginning students, of course, many of the tempos must be slow until the exercises have been learned and coordination is established.

As Barton Mumaw writes: "To the end of his days, Ted Shawn disliked the term 'modern.' He believed that dance should not be arbitrarily labeled old-fashioned or up-to-date, classical or avant-garde. The Denishawn technique had drawn on a wealth of movement sources and dance styles and also incorporated concepts from the teachings of Jacques-Dalcroze and Delsarte. Indeed, Shawn had undertaken considerable research into Delsarte's work and had become a specialist on the subject. Shawn aimed for balanced training exercises involving individual parts of the body as well as coordinated whole body sequences.

The Fundamental Training Exercises have always impressed me in that while they are not technically difficult they become, with knowledge and training, filled with potential and meaning. They are like a seedbed of inspiration for many different kinds and qualities of movement; they provide a basis for development, variation and choreographic experiment for teachers and students, as well as established dancers."

Shawn's concern with developing qualities of movement in students can be seen in the series Tension and Relaxation, Set I and Set II. Tension is a very necessary part of the dance, yet the word is too often given a negative connotation. Today we would perhaps use the word energized to convey the idea of a part of the body being alive, vital and the focal point of the movement. Degrees of tension vary: a slight heightening can produce a light tension, a tensed fist or an arm may be forceful enough to strike a powerful blow. In dance training, one must encounter the range of possibilities in the use of tension and discover when the different levels are most functional and expressive. In the whole exploration of the use of energy-tension and its opposite, relaxation—one must also investigate the use of flow. In some of the exercises that follow, the state of tension is suddenly arrested; in others it flows on, often dissipating completely. Relaxation is more generally understood, though letting the appropriate muscles go limp and making use of gravity do not always come naturally; thus specific exercises to relax the different parts of the body have been provided.

Delsarte's theories of opposition, parallelism and succession are central to the series of falls presented in section X. Through opposition the weight is held back as the body lowers to the floor so that no loss of balance occurs. Weight transference should be smooth and, in that sense, controlled, although the overall pattern is one of free flow. In the lowering process it is the combination of control of balance of body weight and successions in the body with successive lowering that makes the sequences enjoyable to do as well as rewarding to watch.

I. GENERAL STRETCHING SET

Stretching, lengthening the various muscles in the body, develops the instrument as well as increasing the spatial range, the 'reach space' of the kinesphere in which the body is centered.

I A. Upward Stretch and Horizontal Circling (Without Music)

In this exercise vertical extension is followed by horizontal reaching, then a relaxed bouncing as a recovery from the stretched state.

Stand facing front, feet together and parallel, weight on half-toe, arms straight up overhead. Reach up with right and left arms alternately for 8 counts, as if to touch something just beyond reach. Pull up as high as possible, stretching all the muscles of the body taut, at the same time aligning the chest cavity and the pelvis to attain a vertical line from the toes to the fingertips. While holding the torso in this stretched position, lower the heels and tilt forward from the hips, keeping the body perfectly straight from hips to finger-tips until torso is parallel to the floor. At the beginning of the tilt, the hands may be clasped overhead. Circle the torso horizontally around to the right as far as possible and then to the left, keeping the back flat and parallel to floor and maintaining the straight line from hips to fingertips. After circling to left as far as possible, relax and return to center. Now allow the whole body to drop forward, the hands touching the floor. Bounce gently 6 times, then stretch upward and repeat the whole sequence.

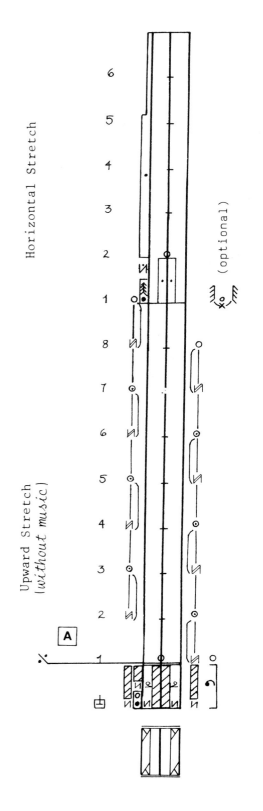

Upward Stretch
(*without music*)

Horizontal Stretch

(optional)

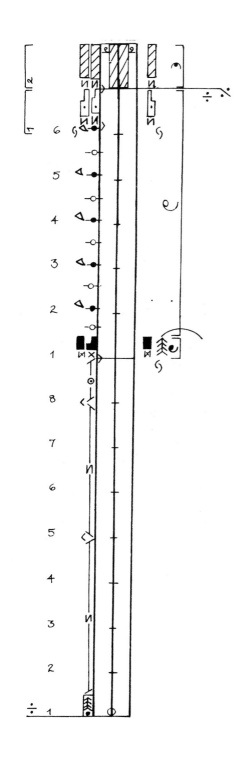

Horizontal Circling

I B. Collapse and Sequential Lift

Part 1: Practice version without music

This exercise provides an early development of the flexible, fluid spine needed for the later, more complex body successions, floor work, etc.

From the lifted position at the end of I A, collapse the torso completely forward. There is a complete relaxation as the body drops forward, as if a balloon had suddenly been pricked and all the air escaped. This is an inward collapse of the torso - an implosion of relaxation. At the same time, the arms fall as if they were a rope held high overhead and suddenly released, and the knees relax and bend. With a gradual increase in energy, slowly return to the erect, lifted position, rising sequentially from the base of the spine, so that each vertebra uncurls in succession, the arms following passively. At the same time the entire front of the torso should be as relaxed as possible and only the back muscles used to recover. This is based on the principle that the solar plexus can remain soft and pliable even when there is strong movement in other parts of the body. The student is advised to test the relaxation of the solar plexus periodically while doing the exercise.

At the peak of the succession of the spine, the arms have arrived overhead. The dynamic of the movement is caused by the total heavy release forward and downward, which is caught at the bottom of the movement by the beginning of the upward succession. Thus from complete relaxation, control takes over and slowly lifts the torso. It is as if the breath was being forced completely out in relaxation and then drawn in with easy control.

Part 2: With music. 8 measures of 4/4

After the ability to keep the abdominal muscles completely relaxed has been mastered, the downward relaxed and upward extending movements are done very swiftly 16 times. The counts are: down 1, up 2, down 3, up 4, and so on. Although performed much faster, the same spinal articulation should be present as in the Practice Version.

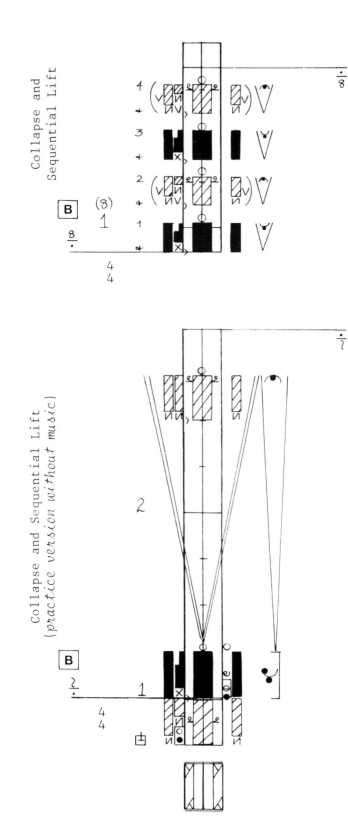

Collapse and
Sequential Lift

Collapse and Sequential Lift
(*practice version without music*)

I C. Torsion Exercise. 8 Measures of 4/4

The central feature of this exercise is the strong torso twist which carries the arms in a horizontal plane.

The Torsion Exercise is executed with a moderate turn-out, the feet fixed firmly in a wide 2nd position, arms stretched out to the sides at shoulder height. The heels remain glued to the floor, as the torso (the unit of pelvis to upper body and head) is twisted alternately to the right and left. The arms, held in one unbroken line from fingertips to fingertips, describe large horizontal circles. There should be no give at the shoulder, thus assuring the utmost torsion. At the same time, the eyes follow the hand in the direction of the twist. Each twist takes 2 counts (4 and 1, 2 and 3). Alternate right and left for a total of eight twists. This pattern then develops into:

Torsion with three-step turn

As you turn to the right, allow the momentum of the arms to carry the body around into a three-step turn to the right ending with the torso twist to the right, as before. Take 3 counts for the turn and one for the twist. Alternate sides for a total of 4 times.

I D. Twist with Limp Wrap-around. 8 Measures of 4/4

The same exercise as I C, is now performed at a slightly slower tempo with the arms completely relaxed and thrown outward from the shoulders during the twist, ending curled like limp ropes around the body. No active arm movement takes place, the spatial shapes for the arms are a passive reaction to the body twist; thus, the feeling for passive, resultant movement is introduced. The counts are: 4 and 1, 2 and 3, etc., for a total of eight twists. Then the three-step turn pattern is performed with the arms strongly held out to the sides at shoulder height during the steps before the 'limp rope' ending; perform 4 times alternating sides.

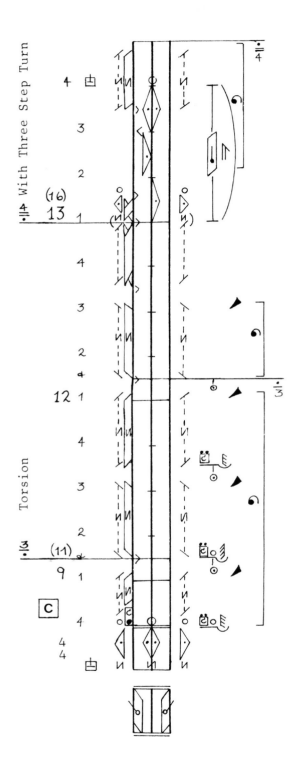

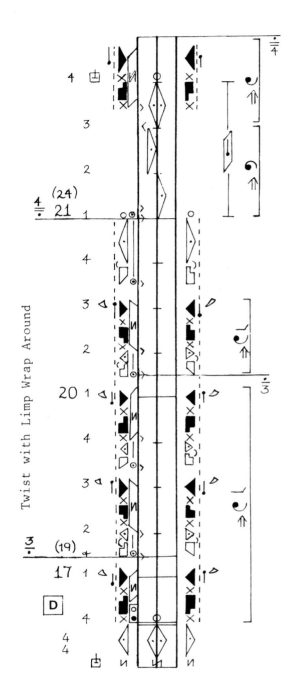

I E. Lateral Arc and Stretch. 16 Measures of 3/4

The circling in this sequence starts into the lateral body direction and then, as the turn takes place, blends into a sagittal arc. Spatially, the arc is unchanging and continues toward the right side of the room. A combined body and space awareness should result from the exercise.

Face front in a wide 2nd with moderate turn-out, the arms stretched out to the sides at shoulder height. With the left arm reach up and over to the right in a complete arc in the lateral-vertical plane of the body. At the same time bend the right leg, shifting the weight to the right and dropping the right arm to the side of the body. Stretch the left side of the torso as far as possible (still flat in the vertical plane), then turn the whole torso 1/4 to the right, continuing to bend over the right leg to look at the floor, bringing the torso parallel to the floor. Bending the right leg as much as possible, touch the floor with the left arm stretched to its full length. Then, from the left foot, begin to pull up through the torso against the pull of the left arm, causing the body to turn left until the torso is again facing front in the starting position, the wide 2nd position, both legs straight, left arm out to the side. The right arm then reaches up and over to the left in an extended arc, repeating the exercise to the other side. Arcing over to the floor takes one measure; the return also takes 1 measure.

Once mastered, this pattern should become a successive movement with special attention given to the extended reaching movement of the arc which causes a complete stretch of the torso.

The Labanotation gives the standard directional description using the stance key to maintain the direction of the arc, but the circular pattern is also described (written on the right of the staff) as a lateral circular path which retains its spatial orientation.

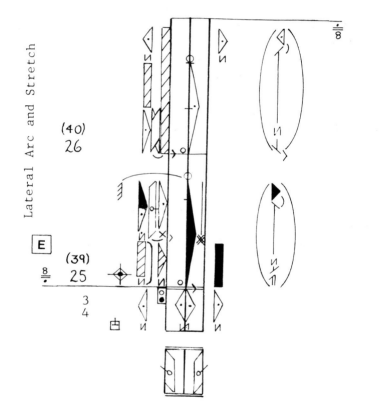

I F. Sagittal Circles. 8 Measures of 4/4

This sequence focuses on articulation in the pelvis, progressing from a small, isolated sagittal circular shift to involvement of the whole body.

Stand feet together, parallel, facing stage right. Beginning with a slight backward shift of the pelvis, make a very small backward sagittal circle (as if the coccyx is drawing the circle). The pelvis circles back, down, forward and up, 1 measure. To accomplish a completely circular movement with the same degree of downward and upward movement, pliability in the knees is important. As the circle is repeated, the size increases, the knees bend more and more, and the circling develops until the entire spine and upper body are involved and bring the arms into play. As the body and arms become fully involved, the movement develops into a swing backward of the arms as the body drops forward, and a swing forward of the arms as the body rises. The final, largest circle is achieved by pushing from the feet, ankles, knees and hips successively into the forward movement; the arms follow the circular pattern of the pelvis, ending overhead.

For each of these circles there is an arpeggio in the music (1 measure). These increase in volume until the eighth and final circle which includes the entire torso, after which the music changes to a waltz for the next development.

I G. Sagittal Body Swing and Succession (Body Wave). 16 Measures of 3/4

Coordination of the whole body with use of weight (gravity) and uplift is the aim of this sequence.

Start facing front, feet together, parallel, on half-toe, body stretching upward, arms overhead. Drop the body forward and down with a feeling of weight, at the same time letting the arms swing forward and down, past the feet to backward horizontal. As the arms move backward horizontal, the torso stretches forward horizontal and the performer rises on straight legs to half toe with a feeling of uplift, of buoyance. This swing takes 1 measure, and is followed by a similar swing down and forward, torso and arms extending forward horizontal (1 measure). A second swing down and back is the preparation for a sagittal succession through the whole spine. For the sagittal succession, push the knees and hips forward and allow the succession (body wave) to include the arms and head. Return to the starting position (2 measures). Perform the sequence 4 times.

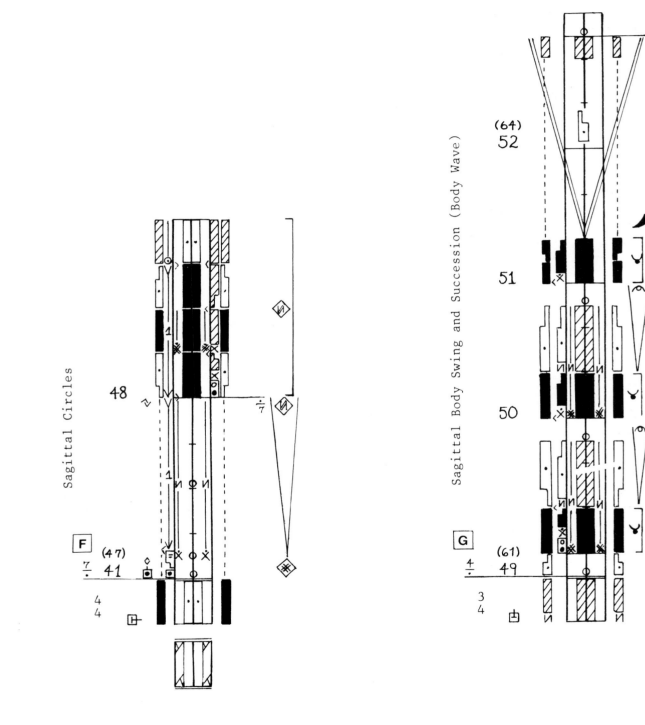

I H. Hip Relaxation. 4 Measures of 4/4

The focus here is on movement of the single hip, in contrast to the pelvic girdle. Because the pelvis is the unit in which the hip sockets are located, one hip cannot be displaced without affecting the other. However, attention can be focused on the action of one hip, as in this exercise in hip isolation.

Start with moderate turn-out, the right leg out to the side, the ball of the foot touching the floor, weight entirely on the left leg. The right hip relaxes and falls downward completely loose in its socket. From that relaxed position, the right hip moves in a lateral circular path as if the hip itself is the only moving part. The leg, ankle and foot are completely relaxed. The leg moves only as a result of the hip action, the foot sliding in and out on an elliptical path. Seven complete circles of the hip are followed by two stamps on the flat of the right foot. The first stamp takes on no weight (a stomp), the second is a step on the right foot which frees the left leg to extend sideward ready to perform the exercise to the other side. Repeat the whole sequence with the left hip.

It is important that the two stamps be done with the full flat foot and with force; a tentative stamp stings and sometimes bruises the foot.

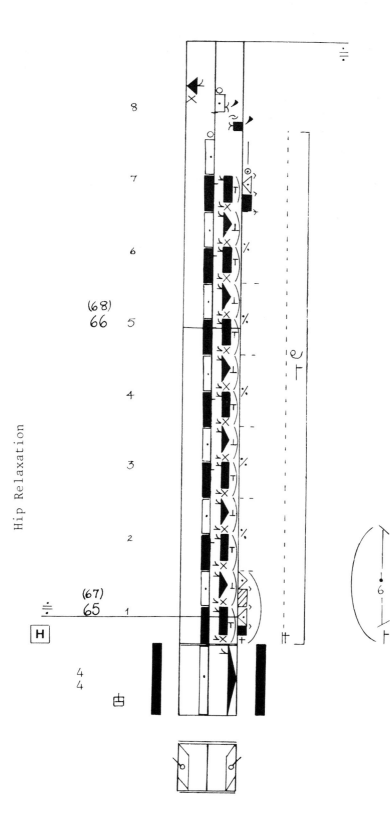

Hip Relaxation

I I. Springs. 8 Measures of 2/4

This exercise warms up the feet for bigger jumps. Keeping the knees straight during the first fast springs uses the metatarsal arch; as the pace slows, the knees bend, and higher, slower jumps result.

Face front, feet together, moderately turned out. The springs in 1st are done with straight legs after an initial elevation from a *plié*. From then on the lift comes entirely from the foot. The tempo becomes progressively slower as the jump becomes higher and the knees begin to bend.

I J. Leg Relaxation. 8 Measures of 4/4

The relaxation exercise which follows the springs is a pawing motion of the entire leg to achieve a relaxed shaking out of the muscles, as if each muscle were hanging loose in its own encasement.

Alternate four pawing movements of the right leg (1 measure) with four pawing movements of the left. Then relax the entire body, bending all the way forward, and shake the body and arms until the end of the music (4 measures). Recover to standing in silence (the last half measure).

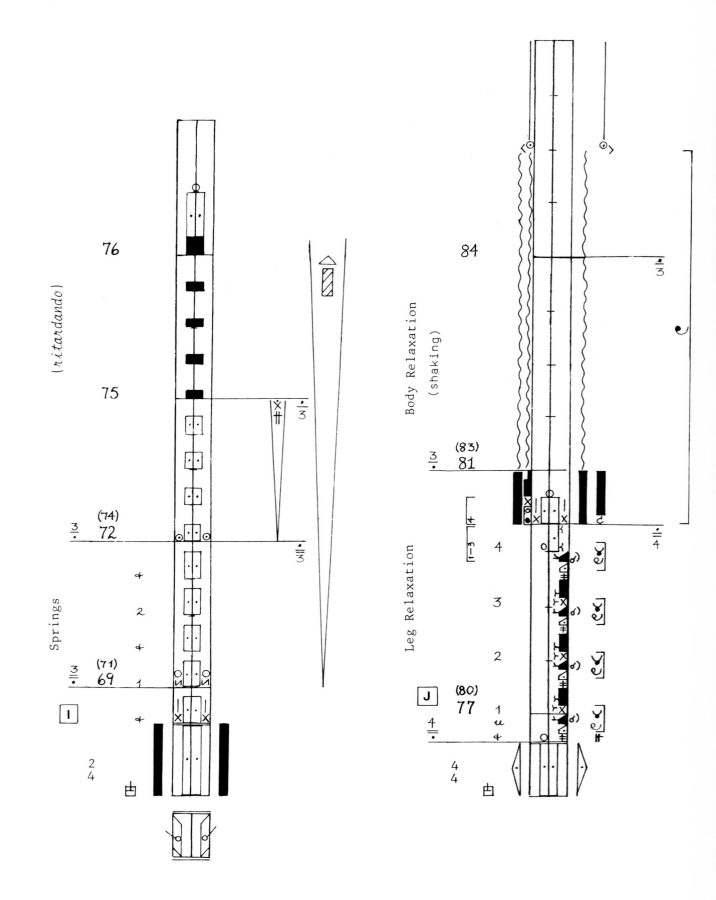

I K. Gnossienne Movement. 14 Measures of 2/4

This sequence, taken from Shawn's solo of the same title, is a good spring-board for discussion of parallel movement - one of the three elements of movement according to the Delsarte theories. The movements demand clear spatial placement of torso and limbs, and quick, separated actions of knees, ankles and feet. It features sharpness of movement and clearly established positions.

Stand in profile, facing right, feet parallel in a small 4th position, right foot some six inches in front of the left. The chest remains facing front for the entire sequence. Twist the chest to the left to face front, keeping the hips still in the profile position. The arms are crooked at the elbow, the left out to the left, fingers together, with the palm open and flat facing front, the hand pointing sideward, bent at the wrist, and with thumb separated and extended. The right arm, also crooked at the elbow, is brought across the chest, the hand in the same position as the left hand and parallel to it. The palm of the right hand faces backward, the arm pressed close to the body. The arms produce the square root sign of mathematics.

On count 1 the knees are sharply bent by the action of the feet rising to extreme half-toe. On the 'and' count the heels return to their original position as the knees straighten. The upper body remains in position and motionless. There should be no rise and fall of the torso in height; all up and down action of the feet is compensated for by the action of the ankles and knees. Four knee actions are performed to the right, and then with a half swivel turn on straight legs, the entire body and arms adjust to the opposite direction for four more knee actions. These are followed by a quick 1/4 turn to face front, with full outward rotation of the legs, the bent arms opening out to each side, hands level with the shoulders and pointing out to the sides, palms flat to the audience and fingers still together. Four similar knee and foot actions occur in this position, then the movements alternate to the right, to the left, and front 5 times, ending the entire exercise facing front.

Shawn in a moment from his dance *Gnossienne*.

This dance was inspired by the Cup Bearer fresco, one of the few remaining on the walls of the ancient Cretan palace of Knossos. For it, Shawn chose the music of the then little-known composer, Erik Satie.

Gnossienne Movement. This classroom exercise in flat two-dimensional style movement was later developed by Shawn into a solo dance.

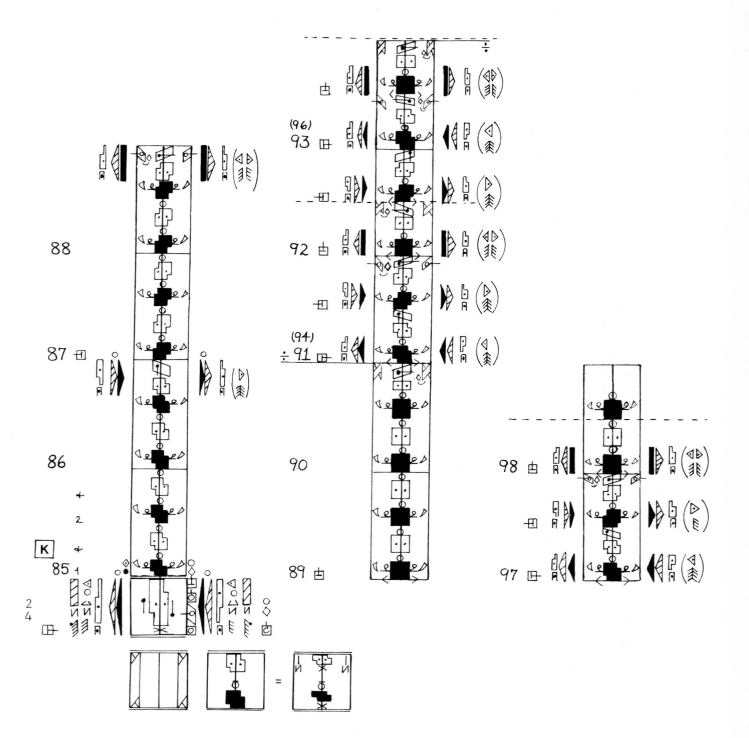

I L. Controlled Balance in Lowering and Lifting. 12 Measures of 4/4

This sequence features slow, controlled movement to be performed with enjoyment of the quality of sustainment, a constant feeling of uplift, and an image of rising even when the body is, in fact, lowering toward the ground. These qualities aid in developing the muscular control needed for slow, fluent movements. Images that assist the performer in mastering this sequence are an awareness of the center line of the body extending up endlessly into space, the idea of this line suspending the body, the upright torso sliding along this vertical line as a bead on a wire.

Face right on high half-toe, feet parallel, the right foot front in a small 4th position, arms overhead, palms facing forward. Keeping the spine lengthened as if on a spindle, take 8 counts to full *plié* slowly, lowering from the base of the spine (center of balance); at the same time gradually lower the arms forward to shoulder level, ending with the palms facing down. Take another 8 counts to rise, lifting from the center of balance to a standing position again on half toe. The arms start to rise with the palms facing up and continue until they are overhead. Conclude with a quick 1/2 turn to the left on the balls of the feet, palms returning to face forward. Repeat to the other side (4 measures). At the end of the second side turn right 1/4 to face front; the legs are now comfortably turned out in a small 2nd position on half-toe, the arms overhead, slightly bent, forming an arch with the palms together. Lower the center of balance, bringing the arms down along the center line past the front of the chest. On counts 7 and 8, turn the hands so that the fingertips point down and the chest leans slightly forward so that the fingers almost touch the floor. Recover at once, fingertips pointing upward, and lift, rising gradually to fully stretched legs, still on extreme half-toe. The arms return to the arched position overhead (4 measures).

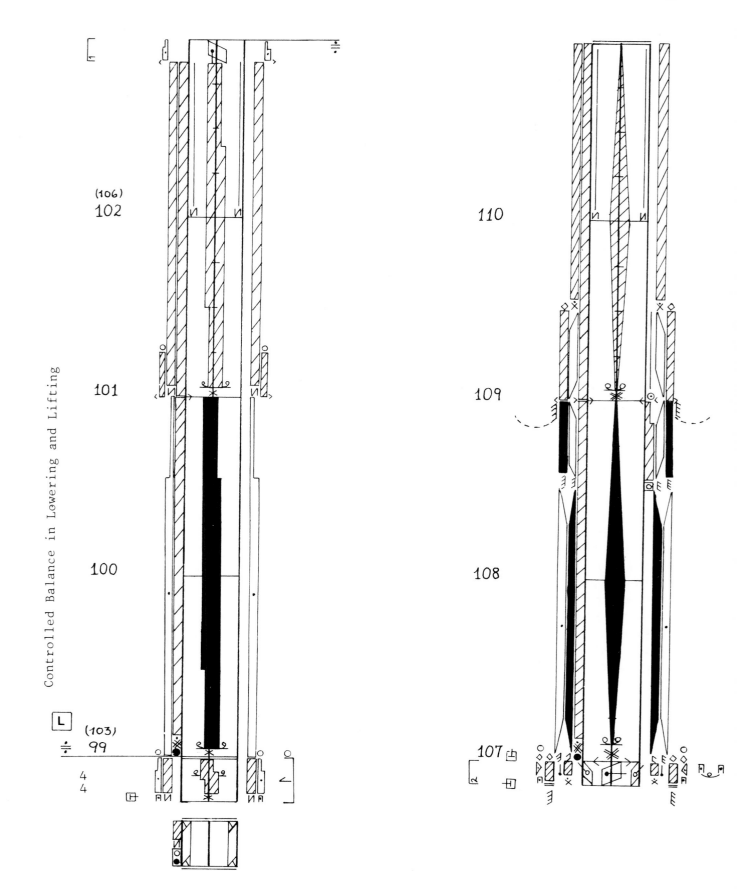

Controlled Balance in Lowering and Lifting

(106)
102

101

100

L
(103)
99

110

109

108

107

II. FIGURE EIGHT SWINGS

48 Measures of 3/4 (Including Material Not Notated)

In contrast to the sustained verticality of the previous exercise, these arm and leg swings feature a flowing sequence in the spatial design of a figure eight. Once the leg comes into play, this exercise also develops balance since one must constantly compensate for the leg's motion. The main directions of the swings - vertical, lateral and diagonal - are the important point, not the precise detail of the execution.

The changes in movement quality which occur in swinging movements have not been indicated in the notation but should be an integral part of the performance. A swing makes functional use of the pull of gravity, the limb relaxing as it moves downward and allowing gravity to take over. Giving in to gravity results in an increase in speed. As momentum causes the limb to rise, the speed decreases and a light control of the path of the limb takes over. Momentum may be almost totally lost at the height of the pattern before the arc begins its downward path and control lessens to allow gravity to take over once again.

Stand with feet together comfortably turned out, arms down. Swing the right arm with body inclusion, using 1 measure to make each loop of the figure eight. The first figure eight is in front of body, perpendicular to the floor, the arm moving high and low. The next figure eight is parallel to the floor, the arms swinging across the front of body to the left, and then out to the right. The next swing is diagonally forward and upward to the left and diagonally backward and downward to the right. Hold for the last 2 measures (8 measures in all). Repeat the above with the left arm (8 measures).

Now repeat with the right arm and the right leg in unison. The figure eights for the leg are: front and back, across to left and out to the right, diagonally left forward high and diagonally right backward low (8 measures).

Repeat with left arm and left leg.

Repeat with the right leg and both arms, the left arm moving parallel to the right arm (8 measures).

Repeat with the left leg and both arms, the right arm parallel to the left one. End with an inward turn to the right (8 measures). These two variations are not given in the notation.

Meas.33 – 48: Repeat meas.17 – 32 to each side
both arms moving parallel and
end with an inward turn to the
right (not notated).

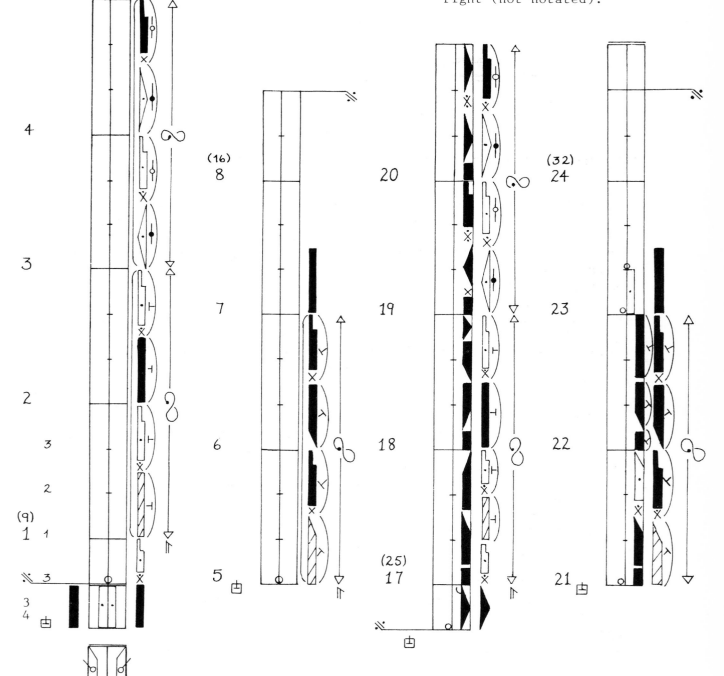

III. TENSION - RELAXATION - SET ONE

Each part of this sequence must be studied and mastered separately before performing it all as a continuous sequence. The Tension-Relaxation exercises emphasize isolated movements of individual body parts, and also inclusion of those parts in movements of other parts. The performer focuses on individual parts in contrasting actions which incorporate first tension, then relaxation. The term 'tension' is used in its positive sense of being energized, forceful.

III A. Head - Tension. 8 Measures of 2/4

Exercises A and B feature isolated head movements, first energetically and staccato, then smoothly, in a relaxed way and legato.

Stand erect facing front, feet together, legs moderately turned out, arms low at the sides, head strongly erect. Snap the head to the right, turning it sharply as if on a pivot, count 1; then snap it to the left, count 2 (1 measure). Repeat 8 times, ending with the head turned to the left.

III B. Head - Relaxation. 16 measures of 2/4

Now with complete relaxation, the top of the head describes a circular path, using 2 measures for a complete circle. The head starts by inclining forward, then rolls around to the right, then backward, and on around to the left. Complete 4 circles (8 measures), and then repeat in the opposite direction. Allow the neck and upper spine to be included in the movement.

III C. Shoulders - Tension. 8 Measures of 2/4

On count 1, sharply raise both shoulders from normal position as if they were going to push right through the skin covering. On count 2, lower them sharply downward as much as possible. Be sure each action is well articulated. Each up and down movement takes 1 measure. Repeat 8 times.

III D. Shoulders - Relaxation. 16 Measures of 2/4

In this sequence, fluent arm circles are the means to achieve relaxation and flexibility of the shoulders.

Starting with the arms down, describe complete circles by moving the arms forward, up, back and down. Take 2 measures to make one circle. The shoulders must be kept relaxed - not easy when making full circles for the whole arm. Perform four circles from front to back (sagittally backward circles) and then four in the reverse direction (sagittally forward circles).

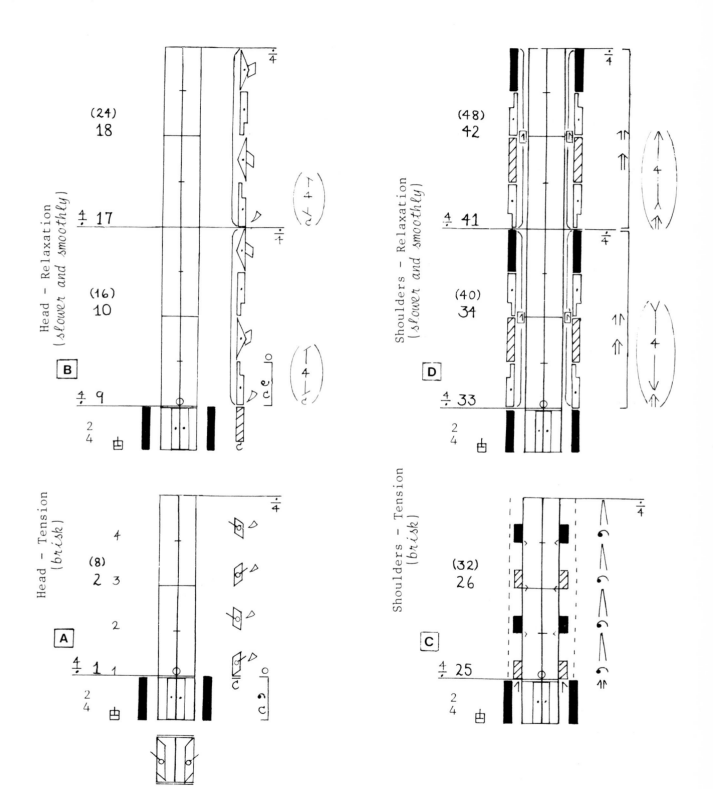

III E. Shoulders - Relaxation. 8 Measures of 2/4

Here horizontal arm swings help increase flexibility in the shoulders.

Starting feet together with the arms out to the sides, palms forward, swing them horizontally to cross in front of the body at chest level, then horizontally out and backward as though to cross them behind the body (1 measure). The arms should be straight but not tensed and the movements should include the shoulders. Repeat 8 times. Aim to touch the backs of the hands together on the backward swing since this provides more opening action for the chest.

III F. Shoulders - Tension. 8 Measures of 2/4

This exercise concentrates on isolation of the shoulder (shoulder blade) in the lateral direction.

Start with the arms sideward horizontal, but slightly forward. Extend the right arm energetically so that the shoulder (and shoulder blade) is pulled out (abducted) as much as possible. Keep it there while the left arm stretches out pulling the left shoulder blade with it. Then bring both shoulders forcibly together (adduction) so that the shoulder blades meet (2 measures). Repeat this sequence 4 times in all, alternating sides.

III G. Hands - Tension. 8 Measures of 2/4

Focus here is on the hands, although the arms participate to augment the movement.

Start with the arms bent forward and near the body, hands in fists. Extend the hands (fingers) forcibly as much as possible, using the arms to help 'throw' them outward. The direction in which the arms extend is not important; different directions may be used. Then contract the arms and hands in preparation for repeating the extension, 8 times in all. Each extension and contraction takes 1 measure.

III H. Hands - Relaxation. 8 Measures of 2/4

Holding the arms out in front, with hands relaxed and hanging down, first shake them up and down to release the tension (4 measures), then circle them laterally outwards (2 measures) and then laterally inwards (2 measures).

Shoulders – Tension
(*steady*)

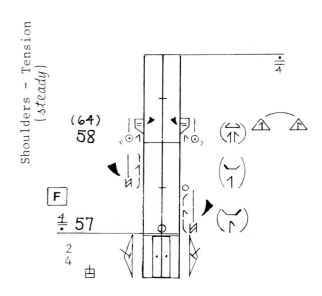

Hands – Relaxation

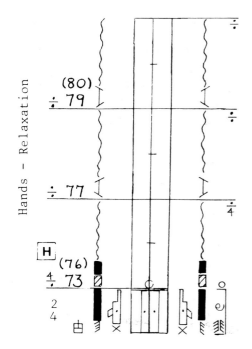

Shoulders –
Relaxation
(*brisk*)

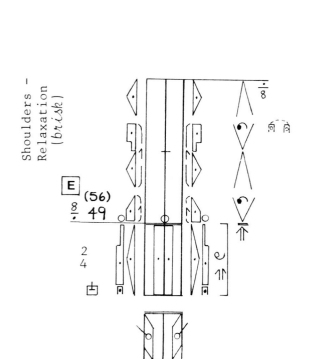

Hands – Tension

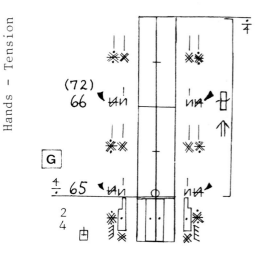

III I. Hip - Tension. 16 Measures of 2/4

This exercise concentrates on sharp isolation of the single hip.

Start feet together, moderately turned out, arms down. Lift the right hip sharply upward so that the foot is lifted entirely off the floor, then smoothly return the hip and leg to their previous, relaxed stance. Lift the right hip 4 times, then the left 4 times (8 measures), then alternate right and left 8 times, at the same time making a complete turn to the right on the spot. The hip action must remain sharp and isolated even though the whole body is turning.

III J. Hip - Relaxation. 8 Measures of 2/4

Hip relaxation is achieved here through flexion of the legs; nevertheless, focus is still on the individual hip.

Start feet together, moderately turned out, hands on hips. On count 1 take a small step to the left on the left foot, bending the knee and allowing the left hip to shift to the left. At the same time, allow the right hip to sag, the right knee falling in toward the supporting leg, the toe still touching the floor. On count 2 return to normal stance with the left hip as high as possible on its supporting leg (1 measure). Repeat to the other side. During the hip drop and recovery a succession occurs through the torso. Repeat alternately a total of 8 times.

III K. Chest - Relaxation (Chest Shift). 8 Measures of 2/4

This exercise involving chest shifts may be performed in a sharp, staccato manner as a chest tension exercise; however, relaxation and a legato performance produce a greater range in such chest isolations.

With the feet together and arms held out sideward horizontal, shift the chest (rib cage) from side to side, starting to the right. Two slow shifts are followed by four quicker ones. These 2 measures are repeated 4 times. The quicker shifts should also be performed with relaxation.

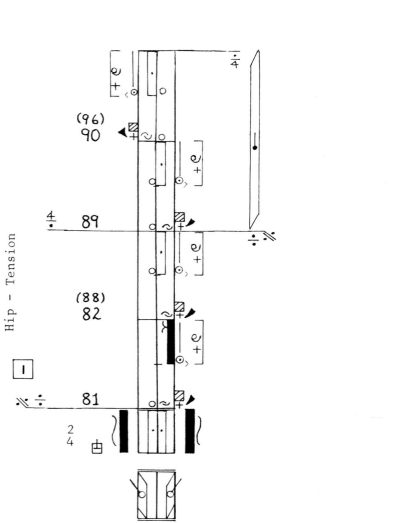

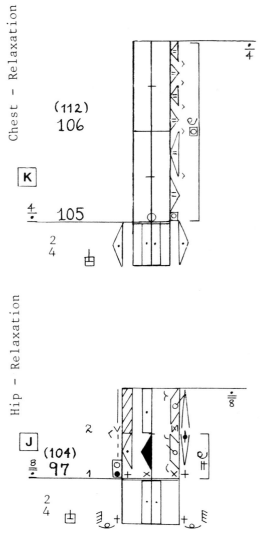

III L. Foot - Tension. 8 Measures of 2/4

While this exercise features foot tension and stretching, the whole leg is actually involved. Some relaxation occurs between each forceful extension.

Start with the feet together, turned out. As a preparation, flex and lift the right leg, bringing the foot in front of the supporting ankle. On count 1 extend and stretch the leg and foot quickly and forcibly forward low, then on count 2 relax the leg and bring it in front of the left ankle. Repeat extending to the side and then to the back. The backward extension is followed by a step backward on the right foot on counts 6 and 7, leading into a repeat of the pattern with the left leg on count 8.

III M. Foot - Relaxation. 8 Measures of 2/4

The shaking action of the leg moves the passive extremity and relaxes it even further.

Raise the right leg and shake the foot loosely for 4 measures, then transfer the weight and shake the left foot. The direction for the raised leg is not important.

III N. Torso - Relaxation and Tension. 6 Measures of 2/4

Start standing upright with the feet together more or less parallel, arms down and relaxed. Shaking the body is initiated by quick, relaxed chest rotations with the arms reacting passively. The torso gradually lowers forward until the fingers almost touch the floor (4 measures). Return to upright through three quick sharp movements occuring on the last three chords of the music.

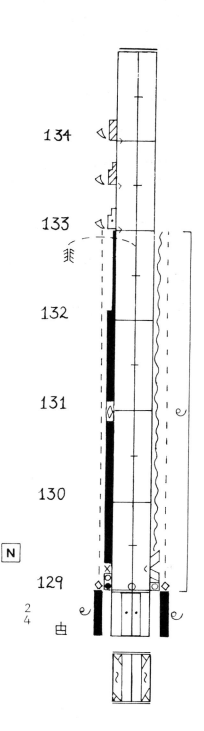

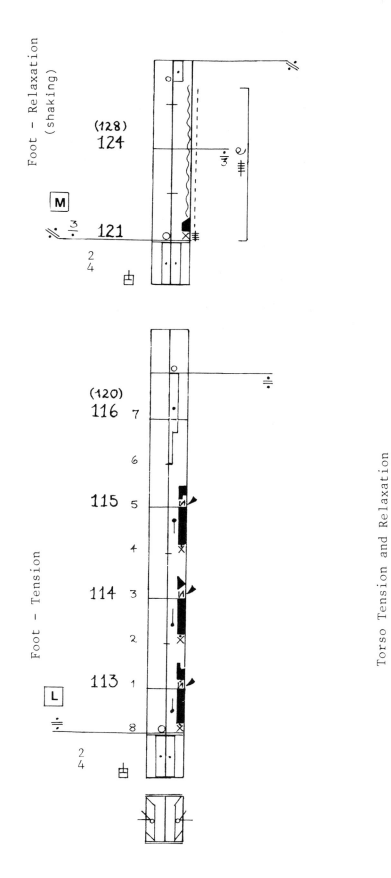

Foot – Relaxation (shaking)

M

(128)
124

121

Foot – Tension

L

(120)
116
115
114
113

Torso Tension and Relaxation

N

134
133
132
131
130
129

IV. TENSION AND RELAXATION - SET TWO

Whereas Tension - Relaxation - Set One comprised a series of individual exercises, Set Two provides connected movement phrases in which the qualities of tension and relaxation are framed in a variety of spatial and rhythmic patterns.

IV A. Tension - Relaxation. 16 Measures of 4/4

This sequence deals with the ebb and flow of energy, setting up a rhythmic pattern of interplay between tension and relaxation in which parts of the body coordinate in unison. A phrase ending is then introduced which features relaxation of a longer duration.

Stand in a circle, facing a counterclockwise line of travel. Begin with feet together, arms forward at shoulder level, bent and with the palms facing down. On count 1 take a high step forward onto the right foot, lifting the left lower leg back just clear of the floor. At the same time tense the whole body - including shoulders, arms, and fists - and incline the head slightly backward. On count 2, bend the supporting leg and release the arms and torso with a slight drop toward the floor, and incline the head a little forward. Draw up through the spine and tense again with another step forward on count 3 and drop again on count 4. Continue for sixteen steps (8 measures).

Repeat the phrase 3 times more, then relax, dropping the torso way forward and, stepping backward with three low steps, let the fingers brush the floor, measures 9 and 10. Repeat these 2 measures 4 times (8 measures).

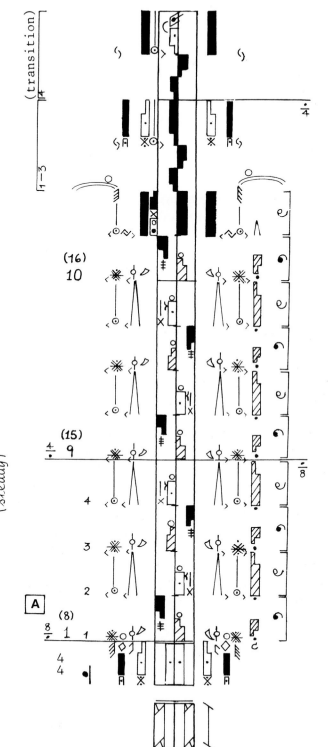

IV B. Zig-Zag Traveling. 16 Measures of 4/4

This sequence highlights relationship to the circle and group awareness. The setting for interplay between tension and relaxation allows for personal variation in direction of limbs; exact spatial placement is not emphasized.

The floor pattern moves diagonally outward from the circle, and then diagonally inward, progressing so that the circle continues to travel counterclockwise.

Turn 1/8 to the right and move away from the center by taking three rising steps forward - right, left, right ending on two feet - at the same time increasing uplift and raising the arms forward and up. Hold the fourth beat with an upward focus and an uplifted feeling. Turn 1/4 to the left to face toward the center of the circle, then take three steps forward to end on two feet, moving progressively lower and becoming increasingly weighty (feeling the weight of the body and limbs). Hold count 4. Moving out and in takes 2 measures. Continue for 8 measures.

The same pattern as the preceding section is repeated but with an increasingly strong quality on the outward and upward movement augmented by the use of the fists, and a heavy and forceful movement incorporating stamps and fists on the downward and inward movement. The sequence ends in a body twist to the left, arms across the body (8 measures). The transition to the next exercise requires a spring turning left to face the center of the circle.

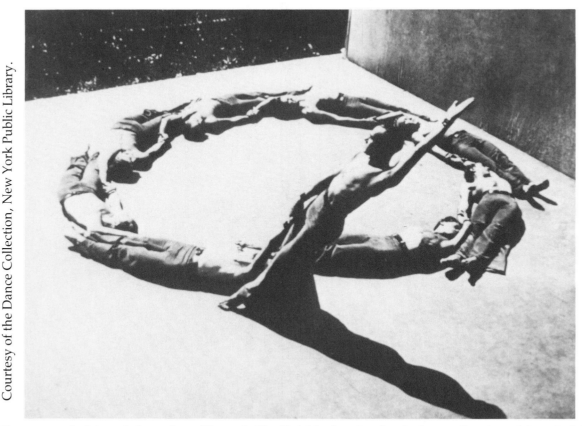

The moment pictured above from Shawn's *Kinetic Molpai*, a circular design ending in a rising straight line, gives a visual representation of the circular form used as a setting for the progressions in the series of exercises in Set Two of Tension and Relaxation.

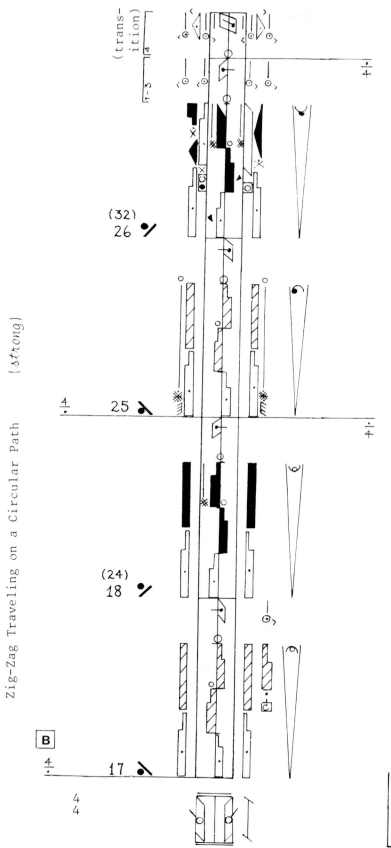

Zig-Zag Traveling on a Circular Path   (*strong*)

IV C. Sideward Springs. 8 Measures of 4/4

Tension and relaxation very closely linked produce a rebound as in these light, resilient springs in which the whole foot is articulated on both the take-off and landing. The lifted, bent knee pushes swiftly upward and produces a comfortably turned out prancing step that prepares the student for learning the pas de chat *step of ballet.*

Facing the center of the circle, arms out to the sides, perform a springing pattern traveling to the right. Both legs are turned out as much as possible. Spring onto the left leg, the right knee out to the side and the foot in front of the left leg (a *retiré* position), count 1. Next spring to the right side onto the right leg, the left being raised in *retiré* in front of the right leg, count 2. The action of knee, foot and ankle should be sharp. Repeat for a total of thirty-two springs.

IV D. Gliding Walk. 8 Measures of 4/4

In contrast to the vertical springing of the previous sequence, this section features smooth, horizontal traveling. The body is held in a high, light tension as if walking on air. Like IV B, this sequence provides training in group formation and the awareness necessary for dancing with other performers.

Turning 1/4 left so that the center of the circle is on your right, walk backward with legs parallel on the line of the circle, arms forward horizontal on the first step. The steps (one to each beat for 8 measures) should be very smooth and flowing so that the upper body is not disturbed at all. On the eighth measure the third step backward is performed with a 1/2 turn right to face into the line of travel of the circle. Close the feet and bend the knees on count 4; the legs are now turned out again in preparation for the next sequence.

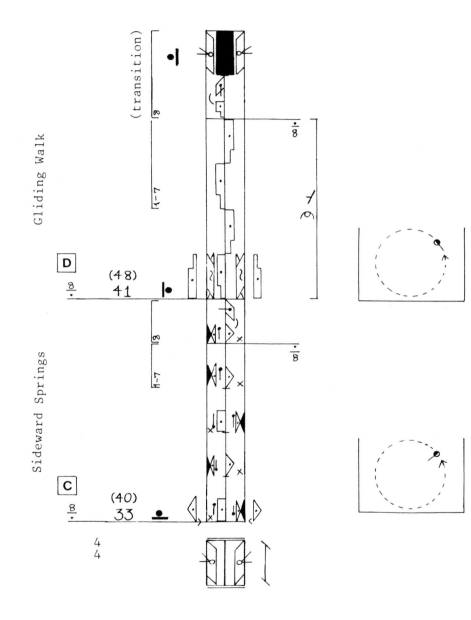

IV E. High Jumps Leading into Running. 14 Measures of 4/4

The small jumps rebounding away from the floor are now enlarged to major jumps using full energy. The running steps in this sequence provide a respite from the high energy needed for the jumps.

Continuing from the previous exercise with the center of the circle at your left, perform a series of jumps in place with the legs turned out. On the first jump spring up on count 1 with the legs pulled up under the hips as high as possible, the feet touching. At the same time bend the torso forward and thrust the arms straight down toward the floor, the hands used as fists. Land on count 2, with the torso upright, arms pulled in and the hands held normally. The jump on count 3 is into a sideward split, the torso inclined forward, the arms out, hands touching the feet if possible. Land feet together on count 4, arms again pulled in. Repeat these two jumps, then, with 1/2 turn left and the center of the circle on your right, take 7 running steps forward, arms down. End with a small spring turning 1/2 to the right and land feet together ready to repeat the whole sequence of 4 measures twice more (12 measures). On the fourth repeat of this jumping sequence the running steps are away from the center of the circle and become the start of the conclusion of this exercise.

IV F. *"Pas de Poisson"* Jumps Ending with Backward Fall. 5 Measures of 4/4

With your back to the center of the circle, take four running steps away from the center (1 measure). Then, closing the feet and bending the knees on count 1, spring into a high *pas de poisson*; the legs joined together move diagonally back left, the chest arches diagonally backward left, and the arms lift diagonally right forward and upward. Land on count 4 on both feet, immediately spring with a 1/4 turn right and run four steps to the center of the circle. Repeat the *pas de poisson* but this time land only on the right foot, tucking the left behind the right leg as a preparation for a sequential backward fall. The final explosion of energy in the last *pas de poisson* is followed by a total collapse onto the ground. Finish the fall with arms extending backward and the legs forward. The dancers' bodies ray out from the center of the circle, providing a choreographed grouping to conclude the whole section.

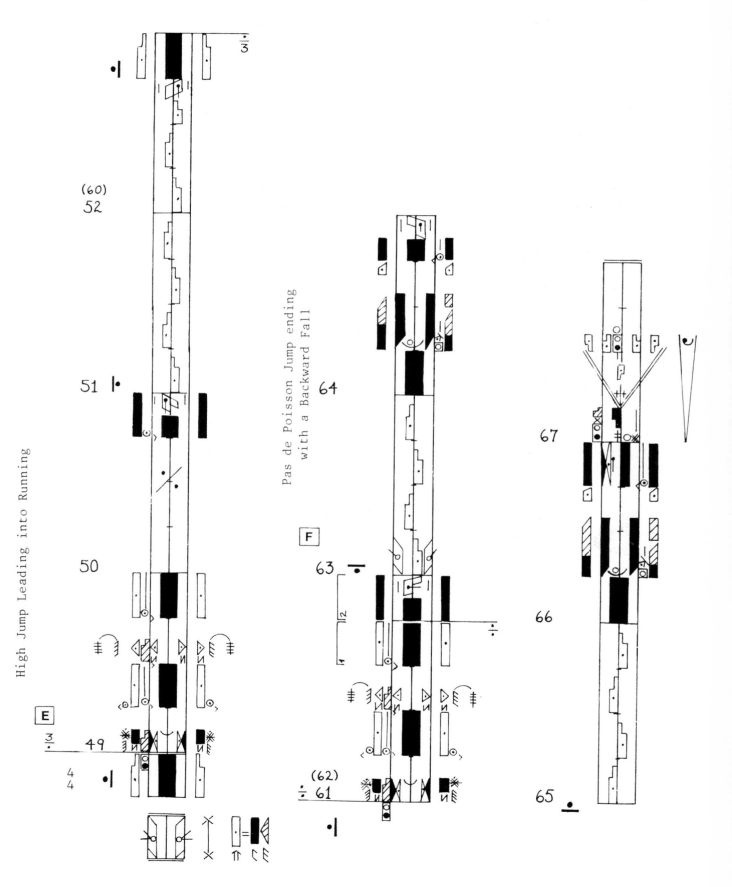

High Jump Leading into Running

Pas de Poisson Jump ending with a Backward Fall

V. FLOOR SET

80 Measures of 3/4

The overall aim of this entire Floor Set is to develop the fluidity in the spine necessary for successional torso movements and expressive spinal articulation.

V A. Back Exercise (The Cat). 8 Measures of 3/4

Kneel facing stage right on 'all fours', hands on the floor, fingers toward each other. The body from knees to hands forms a rectangle. Hands and knees remain in place during this sequence. Begin lowering by taking the hips backward, then, with the back as elongated as possible, push the torso far forward leading with the top of the head; the nose and then the chest nearly brushing the floor, 1 measure. Arching the back toward the ceiling as convex as possible, pull the hips all the way backward, ready to repeat the whole sequence again, 1 measure. Repeat this sequence 4 times. Conclude with a 1/2 turn roll over to the left into a sitting position.

V B. Backward Roll. 8 Measures of 3/4

Sit facing left, back rounded, knees up under chin, hands holding legs tightly together. Roll backward on the spine up to the shoulders, each vertebra touching the floor one after the other, 1 measure. Roll forward into the original position, 1 measure. Repeat 4 times (8 measures). End the last roll sitting, legs spread sideward as wide as possible, hands grasping the ankles, the torso inclined forward.

V C. Resilient Bending. 16 Measures of 3/4

From the stretched, seated position at the end of V B, bend forward and touch the forehead to the floor on count 1. Then, maintaining the rounded torso, lift slightly on counts 2 and 3, (the music is faster here). Repeat 16 times, then as a transition to the next exercise, bring the soles of the feet together with the hands grasping the ankles, torso upright.

V D. Sequential Body Bends. 8 Measures of 3/4

With an inward sequential movement of the spine (i.e. from the extremity to the base), lower the head to touch the feet, 1 measure. Return to the upright position with an outward sequential movement through the back, ending with a backward arch of the rib cage, 1 measure. Repeat 4 times.

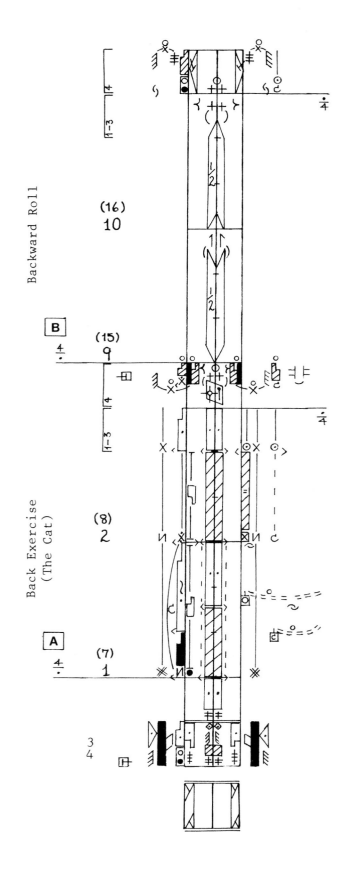

Backward Roll

(16)
10

B

(15)
9

Back Exercise
(The Cat)

(8)
2

A

(7)
1

3
4

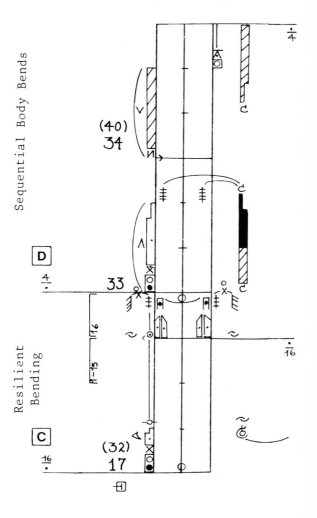

Sequential Body Bends

(40)
34

D

Resilient
Bending

33

C

(32)
17

V E. 'Monkey Roll.' 8 Measures of 3/4

With the spine rounded forward, soles of the feet still together and hands still grasping the ankles, roll onto the right side of the body, around onto the back and onto the left side and then roll up to sitting, the torso still rounded, 2 measures. Repeat this circling in the same direction (clockwise), then repeat twice rolling and circling the other way. At the conclusion return to sitting facing front, weight only on the hips, the legs off the floor, parallel and bent in front of you, knees together, arms out to the sides, torso tilted backward high as a counterbalance.

V F. Hip Roll into Full Roll. 16 Measures of 3/4

With only the hips touching the floor, rotate the pelvis to the right and roll onto the right hip, the right arm swinging left across the body to aid balance. Rotate the pelvis to the left and roll onto the left hip, the left arm moving to the right. Then roll completely around to the right, extending the legs and arching the back with the arms beyond the head in order to keep legs and upper body off the floor. End in the starting position, 4 measures. Do this sequence 4 times alternating sides.

As a transition into G, roll back into a shoulder stand, legs and torso up to the ceiling, arms out sideward on the floor to aid balance.

V G. Shoulder Stand. 16 Measures of 3/4

Hold the position for 4 measures keeping as vertical as possible. Then bicycle (sagittal leg circling) for 4 measures. Still in a shoulder stand, touch the floor behind the head 6 times, first with the right foot, then the left, keeping legs straight (6 measures). Roll forward to sitting position, legs crossed, the right in front, torso rounded, arms by your side (1 measure), and rise at once into *attitude* without using the hands to help get off the floor (1 measure). Allow the roll to propel you into standing.

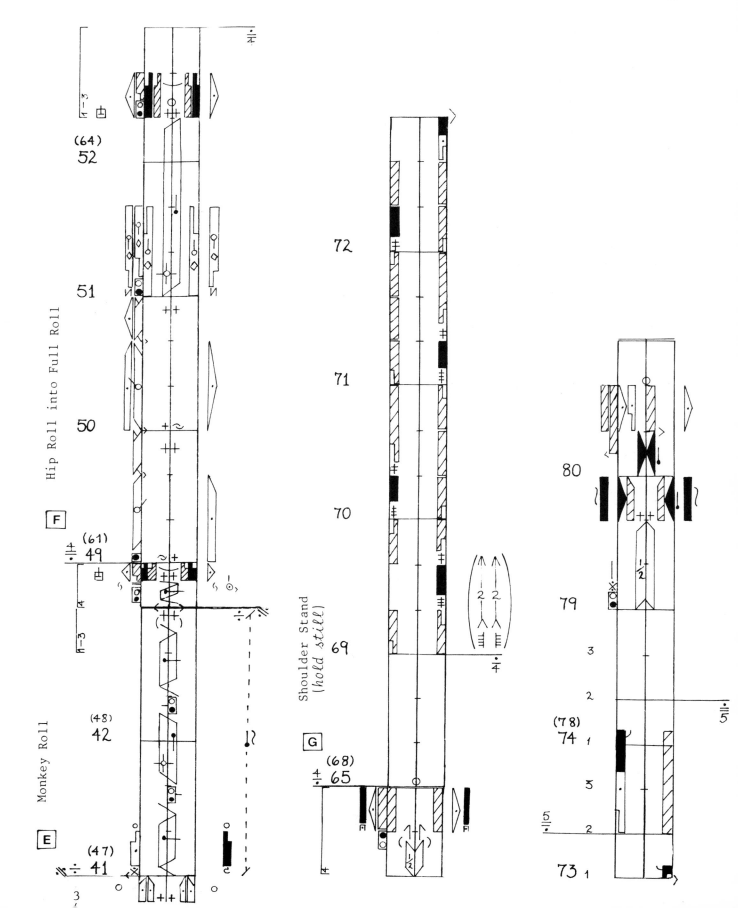

(64)
52

51

Hip Roll into Full Roll

50

F

(61)
49

Monkey Roll

(48)
42

E

(47)
41

3

72

71

70

Shoulder Stand
(hold still)

69

G

(68)
65

80

79

3

2

(78)
74

5

2

73

VI. THREE JUMPS

12 Measures of 2/4

The vigorous jumps which follow must only be attempted when the body is thoroughly warmed up. Depending upon the students' technical level and ability to jump high, the music may need to be slower or faster.

VI A. Sideward Jump. 4 Measures of 2/4

Stand erect, facing front, feet together, legs parallel. *Plié* on count 1, then jump into the air on count 'and', bending the knees sharply and keeping them close together while the legs rotate to the right so that both lower legs point horizontally to the left. At the same time, with both hands held in fists, carry the left arm straight out from the shoulder, while the right arm quickly circles outward and upward to end curved overhead as the body arches strongly to the left. The arms retrace their path and end with body erect on the landing, count 2. On count 'and', repeat the jump to the other side. Perform eight jumps (4 measures).

VI B. In and Out. 4 Measures of 2/4

Continuing without a break from the previous sequence and using the same timing, jump into the air, drawing the feet up until they touch, knees out to the side. At the same time the arms, starting near the chest, reach downward towards the floor with fists together, touching the ankles of the drawn-up feet. Land and jump straight up again opening the legs out to each side and bending forward from the waist to touch the feet with the hands. It takes 2 counts to complete two jumps. Repeat 3 more times (4 measures).

VI C. Front and Back. 4 Measures of 2/4

Without a break from the previous sequence, jump into the air, body bent slightly forward and knees together bent sharply up in front, at the same time slapping the tops of the thighs. Land and jump up again, bending the legs sharply backwards and arching the body backward as the palms slap the soles of the feet. Perform this sequence 3½ times, landing after the spring with legs forward and parallel, feet close together, knees forward and the torso extended forward high with arms backward horizontal, a position similar to a racing start for a swimmer.

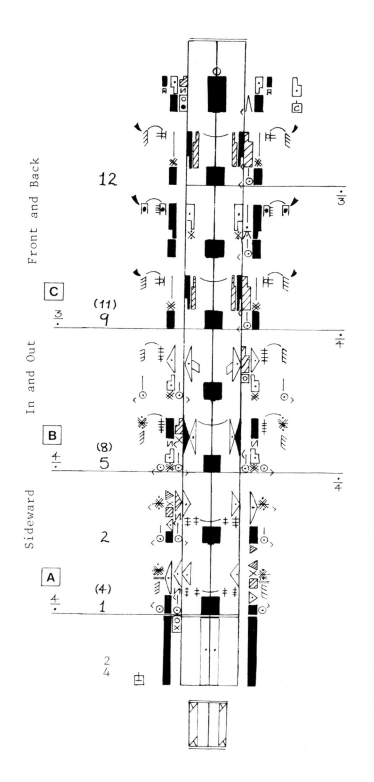

VII. WALKING, RUNNING, LEAPING

80 Measures of 4/4

This series begins with simple controlled transferences of weight. Gradually the tempo of the movement increases and the sequence progresses around the room, leading into springing steps and finally into leaps; the arms are used first in natural opposition, then are raised overhead for the subsequent turning leaps.

VII A. Overcurve Transference of Weight. 8 Measures of 4/4

This first section develops a smooth, sustained overcurve of the center of the body through controlled foot articulation.

Moving in a circle counter-clockwise, start standing erect with the right foot forward, toe touching the floor, the legs in a comfortable turn out. Rise straight up to half-toe on the left foot, leaving the right toe on the floor, count 1. Shift the weight smoothly forward onto the right foot, still on half-toe, count 2. Lower forward to the whole foot, all the weight now transfered to the right foot, count 3, the left foot remaining touching in back, and hold count 4 (1 measure). Rise onto half-toe on the right foot, count 1. Shift the weight backward onto the left foot on half-toe, count 2. Lower to the left whole foot, all the weight now transfered to the left, count 3; hold, count 4 (1 measure). Perform this sequence a total of 4 times.

VII B. Continuous Overcurves. 4 Measures of 4/4

At a slightly faster tempo, make the forward and backward transferences of weight a continuous movement so that the pattern becomes more rounded, rising first on both feet and then transfering to one, i.e. a smooth upward arc rather than the angular shape too often performed. Use 2 counts for the forward shift and 2 counts for the backward shift.

VII C. Progressive Overcurves. 4 Measures of 4/4

Note the timing change now to arrival on count 1. At the end of the previous measure, rise and transfer the weight forward onto the right foot, finishing the overcurve on count 1. On count 2 rise to half-toe on the right foot, allowing the left leg to 'swing' through at the height of the movement, end touching the floor in front. On counts 3 and 4, repeat on the other side. Repeat for a total of eight steps.

VII D. Lilting Overcurve Steps. 8 Measures of 4/4

Continue the same step pattern but, as the music increases in speed, the same mechanics of movement become necessarily smaller. In this section one step occurs to each beat. After 4 measures the music becomes even faster so that walking develops into a light, springy run. At the end of this section the music changes to a fast waltz rhythm.

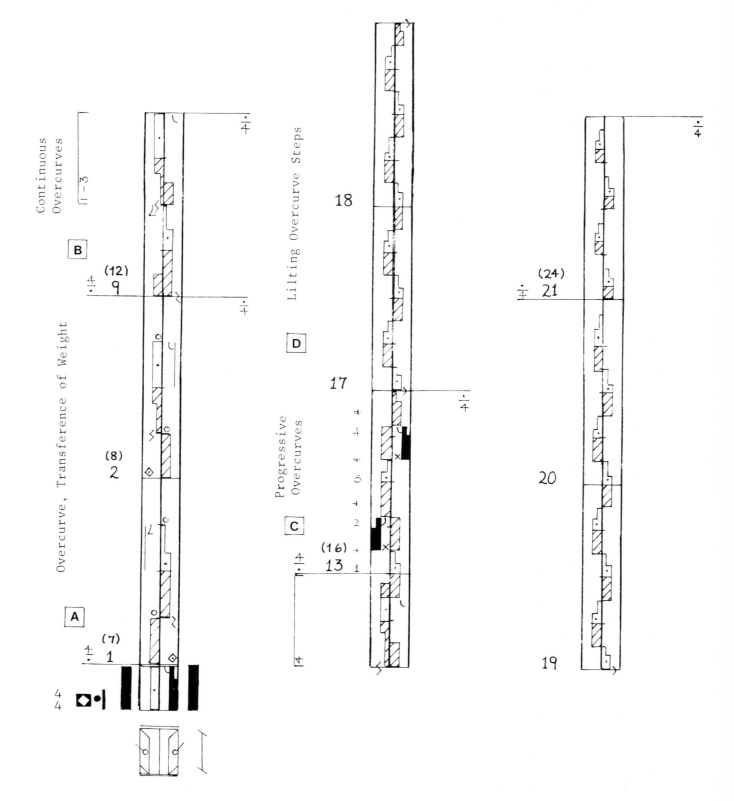

VII E. Springing Runs with Leg Extensions. 8 Measures of 3/4

Continue to travel forward lightly springing from foot to foot, the free leg extending forward low, on a normally straight leg, one spring to the beat. On each spring use a sharp pushing movement of the foot against the floor. Repeat for a total of 8 measures.

VII F. Springing Runs with Knee Lifts. 8 Measures of 3/4

Continue springing one step to the beat but pick up each knee sharply in front as if touching it to the chest, keeping torso upright.

VII G. Springing Runs with Low Leg Lifts. 8 Measures of 3/4

Continue running but now carry the lower legs back and upwards as if to slap them against the buttocks.

VII H. Springing Runs with High Leg Extensions. 8 Measures of 3/4

With an increase in energy spring as in VII E, but with the straight-legged forward gestures lifted as high as possible.

VII I. Leaping Sequence (Two Measure Phrase). 8 Measures of 3/4

The run now develops into a leap landing on count 1, followed by five running steps, the last one acting as a preparation for the next leap, 2 measures. The legs separate sagittally in the air, the arms swinging in opposition. Each leap lands on the right foot.

VII J. Leaping Sequence (One Measure Phrase). 8 Measures of 3/4

With fewer steps between the leaps now land on alternate feet. Land on count 1 of each measure and take only two steps into the next leap. Alternate sides 8 times.

VII K. Turning Leaps (Two Measure Phrase). 8 Measures of 3/4

The same basic pattern as VII J, but changing the physical (body) direction on the second leap while maintaining the direction of travel. On measure 1, leap forward landing on the right, followed by two runs, then leap into the air with a 1/2 turn to the right, landing backward on the left (measure 2). A 1/2 turn to the right while running backward leads into a leap forward again. Continue this pattern alternately forward and back until the seventh measure when, with three steps - right, left, right - all performers run to the center of the circle and, on the last chord, all finish with a step forward on the left, the back leg straight, the right arm extended overhead, the left arm back, shoulder height.

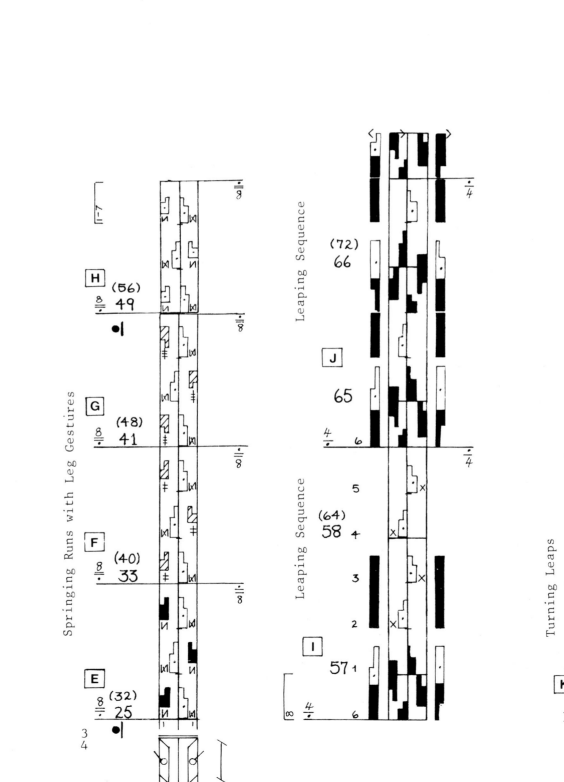

Springing Runs with Leg Gestures

Leaping Sequence

Leaping Sequence

Turning Leaps

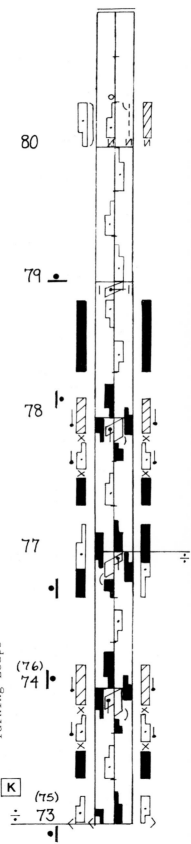

VIII. LONG ADAGIO (BALANCE EXERCISE)

64 Measures of 3/4

Control in slow movements is a necessary challenge for every student. The aim is not only maintaining balance while supporting on one leg but also being able to achieve fluent, sustained movements at the same time. The exercise in balance given here is patterned on a typical balletic adage. *The positions to be passed through or arrived at need to be clear while at the same time there should be a continuous sense of ongoing, of 'parceling out' the movements to fill all the time available. If the leg cannot be carried at full height to begin with, half height should be used so that the quality of sustainment and the simple spatial progressions are not sacrificed. Note the use here of ballet terminology with explanation of the positions provided since terms vary somewhat from one 'school' to the next.*

Stand facing front with legs turned out, feet in 5th position, right foot front, arms in *bras bas* (low 5th, i.e. down, rounded, with the hands in front of the body). With sustained controlled movement, bring the right leg up to the high *passé* position (foot raised to knee), with the arms rising continuously to a low 1st, 4 measures. Without a break extend the right leg straight forward, raising the arms to 1st position (5th *en avant*, i.e. directly in front of the chest), 4 measures. Carry the leg out to the side (*rond de jambe*), arms opening out sideward to 2nd position, 4 measures. Carry the right leg around backward to *arabesque*, moving the arms to 1st *arabesque* (left arm forward, right arm backward), 4 measures.

Flex the right leg, changing it to *attitude*, carrying the right arm in a full *port de bras* down, forward and up, the left arm opening to the side, 4 measures. Extend the right leg and then draw it in to *passé*, bringing the foot in to the standing knee while the right arm opens out to the side to 2nd position, 4 measures. Without a pause, develop the right leg into a forward extension, the arms moving down to low 1st (forward low and rounded), then rising to 1st (5th *en avant*, rounded and in front of the chest), 4 measures. *Relevé* (rise) on the supporting foot as the arms move swiftly to 5th overhead, 1 measure. Drop forward on the right foot into a 4th position lunge while the arms open out to the sides, making a full *port de bras* downward, and end crossed; the torso is rounded forward so that the hands touch the floor, 1 measure. Recover onto a straight leg, weight on the right foot, the left leg making a low, inward circular movement via side (*rond de jambe*), finishing with the left foot front closing into 5th, while the arms open to the side and then lower to the starting position, 1 measure. Repeat on the other side (32 measures).

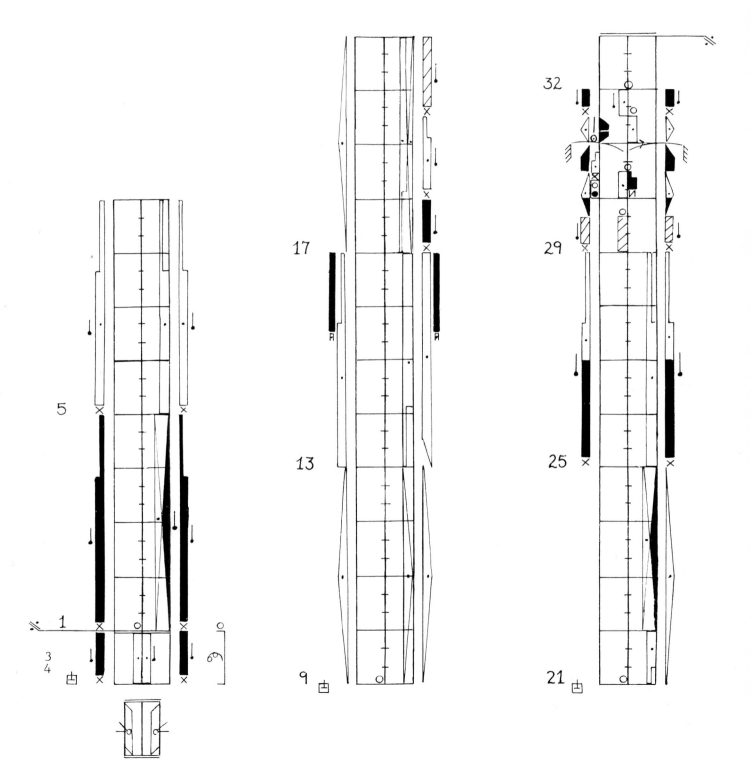

IX. SINGLE ARM SWING AND DEVELOPMENT.

96 Measures of 3/4

Barton Mumaw notes: "Emphasis in this study is on giving the impression that the movement is controlled from outside the body as if from the pull of a natural force, as of the tides, or a magnetic energy to which the body responds with an ever increasing dynamic until it explodes into the leaping circular and spiral movements of the Fifth Development (Section F). This exercise is also valuable in training groups to being able to work closely together. Through its development of a single basic movement idea, it is also a simple example of choreography."

IX A. Basic Pattern. 16 Measures of 3/4

In the basic pattern which precedes the whole development, the swing is initiated by the arm alone; allow it to swing down and up as a result of its own weight. As it swings, allow a slight inclusion of the body to occur.

Face front, standing feet together comfortably turned out. Raise the right arm diagonally back at shoulder level, straight but not tense. Let it swing down and up to the left forward high diagonal. Then let it swing down and up to right back diagonal horizontal, 2 measures. Perform a total of 4 times then repeat with left arm for a total of 4 times.

IX B. First Development. 8 Measures of 3/4

The swing starts very small and gradually increases in size. Relax the shoulder and let the right arm's own weight make the arm swing a little, first diagonally forward left (1 measure), then diagonally back right (1 measure). Repeat for a total of 4 times, gradually increasing the size of the movement.

IX C. Second Development. 8 Measures of 3/4

Now increase the size of the movement even more, adding a slight inclusion and shift of weight as the feet step into the direction of each swing. Repeat for a total of 4 times.

IX D. Third Development. 8 Measures of 3/4

Increase the movement even more by allowing the free leg to lift from the floor after the step on each swing. Repeat for a total of 4 times.

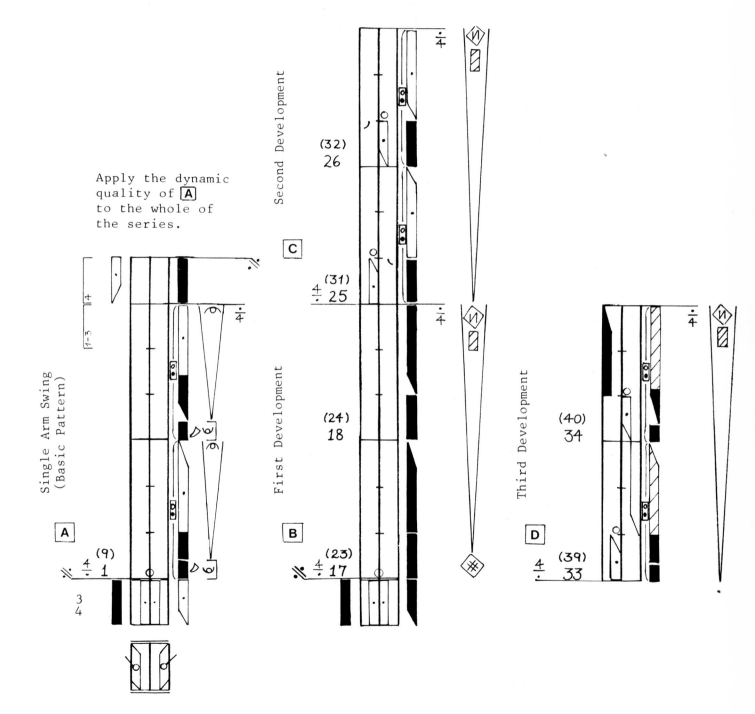

IX E. Fourth Development. 16 Measures of 3/4

The arm is now swinging from high diagonal back to high diagonal forward. After one forward-backward pattern, allow the arm to swing forward, up, back and down in a complete circle ending again diagonally forward high. During this circular pattern take three steps diagonally forward on counts 1, 3, 1. This phrase takes 4 measures. Now reverse the whole pattern, swinging down and backward high, down and forward high, then down and backward high on around in a complete circle to end diagonally back high. During the circle, take three steps diagonally backward (4 measures). Repeat all of this development.

IX F. Fifth Development. 8 Measures of 3/4

Repeat the full arm circle with three steps as in E, but augmenting the movement by turning to the left and rising while traveling on a straight path diagonally forward. This turning results in the circular arm swing producing a spiral pattern overhead. Repeat reversed, turning right and traveling on a straight path backward right. Repeat all of this sequence. During the turning the impetus of the arm may lift the body off the ground. This is not indicated in the notation.

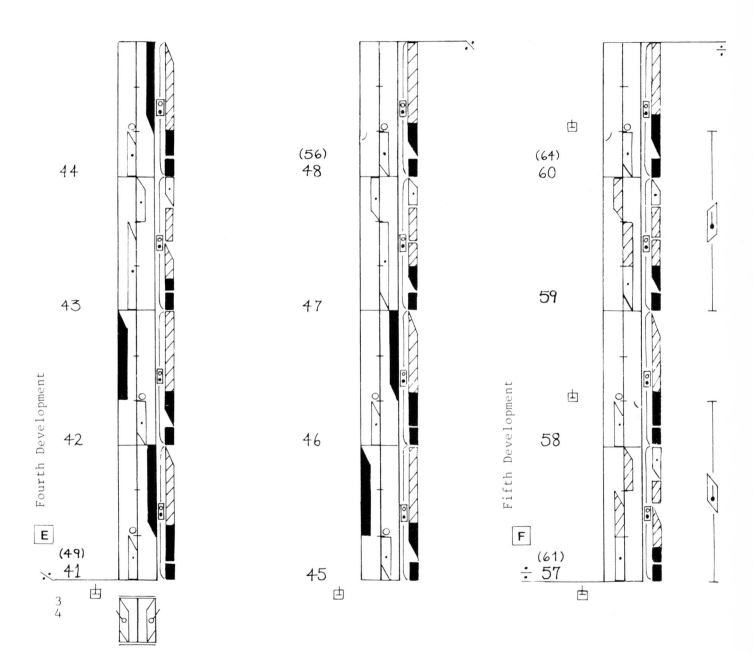

IX G. Sixth Development. 8 Measures of 3/4

Now that the height of the build-up in the arm swing movement is over, the swinging gradually subsides as it continues. Perform the fourth development without the repeat.

IX H. Seventh Development. 8 Measures of 3/4

Diminish the energy and use of space even more in repeating the third development 4 times.

IX I. Eighth Development. 8 Measures of 3/4

Subside to repeating the second development 4 times.

IX J. Ninth Development. 8 Measures of 3/4

The movement now returns to the first development getting continuously smaller and smaller until the body barely moves. The whole sequence of developments should then be repeated to the other side, again first with increasing, then with decreasing range and energy.

When performing this swing and development as a group exercise, the dancers all start close together, facing front. As the movement develops spatially, the group separates enough to allow the arms to pass between each other. The dancers then separate even more to accommodate the turning steps. As the movement subsides the group gradually closes up to return to the starting formation.

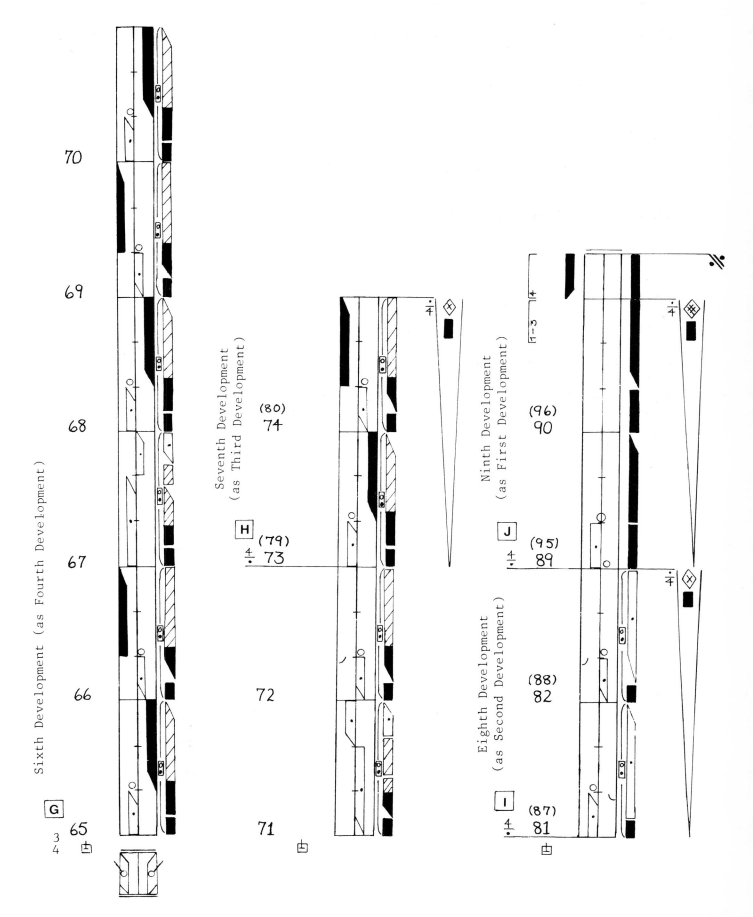

X. THREE DELSARTE FALLS, RISING AND FALLING

24 Measures of 4/4

X A. Spiral Fall. 8 measures of 4/4

Start facing left, feet together with a moderate turn out, arms down. Step back on the right foot and swing the arms back, count 1. Lower as you step forward on the left, swinging the arms forward toward stage left while lowering even more to kneel onto the right knee as you turn 1/4 right to face the audience, count 2. While inclining the chest to the right, take the weight onto the left lower leg and hip at the same time arcing the arms from stage left to overhead and on out to stage right, count 3. With body and arms keeping the weight toward stage right, turn to sit facing stage right, arms and body ending forward, count 4 (1 measure).

Sequentially uncurl each vertebra of the spine onto the floor while lowering the torso backward, legs extending forward. Arms and head are the last to finish uncurling, arms finishing back. The rising which follows takes 2 measures, arms moving sharply up and forward as you come swiftly to a sitting position, count 1. Turning left and facing the audience, but leaving the arms toward stage right, bend the knees and rise onto the left knee, arms trailing across the front of the body on counts 2, 3, 4. Take three steps - right, left, right - in a counterclockwise circle to face right, counts 1, 2 and 3, while the body comes upright and the arms lower. Repeat the fall and rise to the other side (4 measures for the rise and fall, 8 measures in all).

X B. Backward Fall. 8 Measures of 4/4

Start facing stage left, feet together and arms forward. Take a long step back on right foot, twisting the body to the right and swinging the arms downward and across the body toward stage right. Then, untwisting the body, take a long, forward low step on the left foot, carrying the body and arms way forward to counterbalance as, with the entire weight on the left foot, a kneel backward on the right knee leads to sitting backward, the weight of arms and body still held forward until safely seated; then uncurl sequentially backward onto the floor, the legs ending forward, the arms backward beyond the head (2 measures). Sit up with a sharp upward and forward swing of the arms, then leaning forward, cross the legs, the right foot nearest the audience in front. Without using the hands, push up to the feet and untwist as you rise, swivelling 1½ turns to the left to end facing right, the body upright, the arms down. Repeat all of this sequence to the other side (8 measures in all).

Note: This series of falls does not contain falling in the sense of loss of balance, but variations on a swift, smooth lowering to the ground.

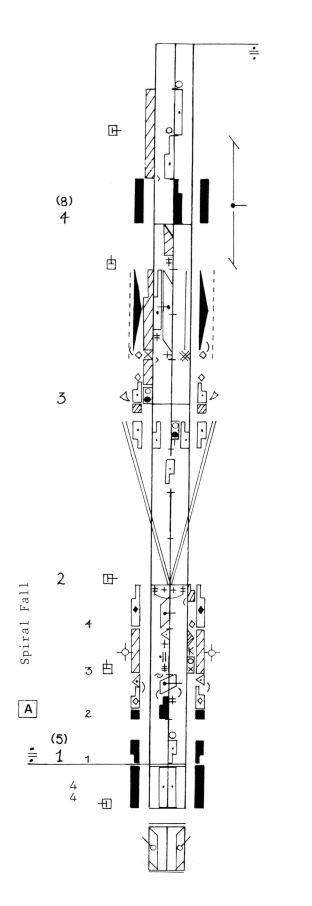

Spiral Fall

A

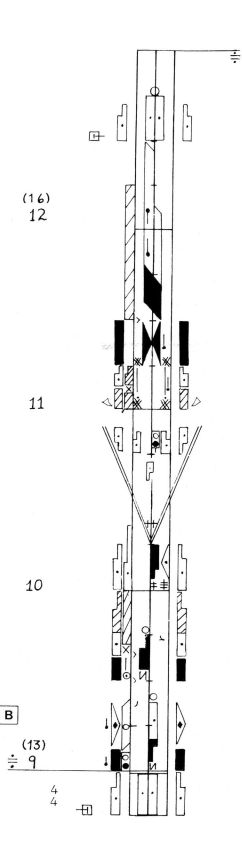

Backward Fall

B

X C. 'Forward' Fall. 8 measures of 4/4

Note that although this exercise is called a 'Forward' Fall, the body direction of the movement is sideward.

Begin facing left. As a preparation step back on the right foot, twisting the torso to the right and swinging the arms across the body toward stage right. The rest of this fall is similar to the first spiral fall, but does not roll over onto the back. Stay on the left hip facing front as the arms move up and across to the right in preparation for unfolding the body to the left into the 'splash' out onto the floor. End on the left side of the torso, the head turned to the left, the face down, resting on the cushion of the left arm (2 measures).

On measure 3 roll over to the right onto the back and then onto the right side of the torso, bringing the right knee up ready to put weight on it. With a little help from the right hand rise to the right knee, then take three steps - left, right, left - circling clockwise to end facing stage right. Repeat to the other side but with the following ending:

After the last fall, do not rise, but roll over to the left and lie face down for the last measure (8 measures in all).

Courtesy of the Dance Collection, New York Public Library.

The extreme pull away from the direction of the 'fall' is illustrated in this photograph of Shawn in a moment from his solo *Frohsinn*. Such counterbalance of weight assures that no actual drop, i.e. loss of balance will take place.

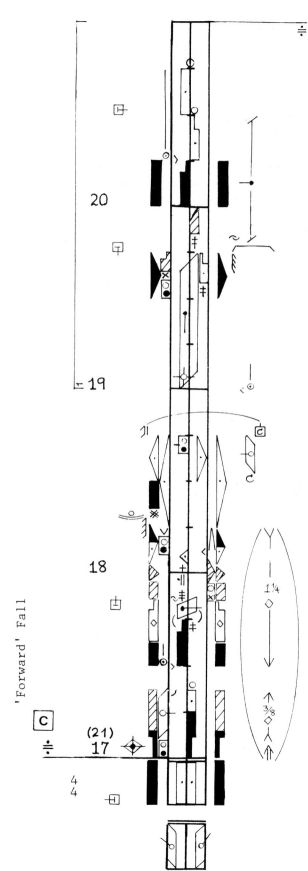

'Forward' Fall

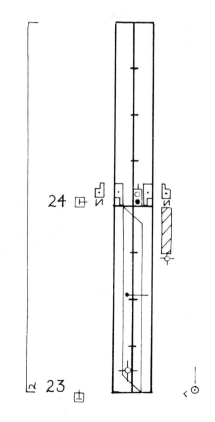

X D. Rising and Falling. 32 Measures of 3/4

Barton Mumaw notes: "This sequence features suspension, that moment between the high point of a movement and its release — the luftpause of a Viennese Waltz, the high note before a falling cadenza, the moment of pause before a wave breaks, the caught breath. At the high point of the rise the relaxation begins in the feet but the torso is still at its apogee."

Continuing from the previous sequence, (lying flat on the floor, face down, head towards stage right, the arms stretched out on the floor in front of the body) on count 1 of the first measure, the hands come in to the side of the chest, fingers facing inward, positioned to lift the torso, toes tucked under to prevent sliding backwards. On counts 2 and 3 of the first measure and all of the second measure, walk the hands backward to the feet; as the center rises upwards, the body bends sharply at the hips, the spine as straight as possible, legs straight and on half-toe. On the third measure unfold sequentially with increasing uplift, pulling up to full height, arms overhead. Suspend there for the fourth measure.

Release the tension and start to turn to the left, torso and arms moving toward stage left (i.e. they start moving in a backward direction from the body). Complete the 1/2 turn ending on the left foot, the right leg tucked across in back in preparation for lowering to a kneel on the right knee, the torso and arms held far forward (1 measure).

From kneeling, sit backward and unfold sequentially to lying, the vertebrae touching the floor one after the other, arms sliding on the floor to end backward (1 measure). Roll over to the left onto the front, limbs extended as in the starting position, ready to repeat the sequence, 1 measure. Hold 1 measure (8 measures for the whole sequence). Perform the rising and falling 4 times, the last time rolling onto the back to finish (32 measures).

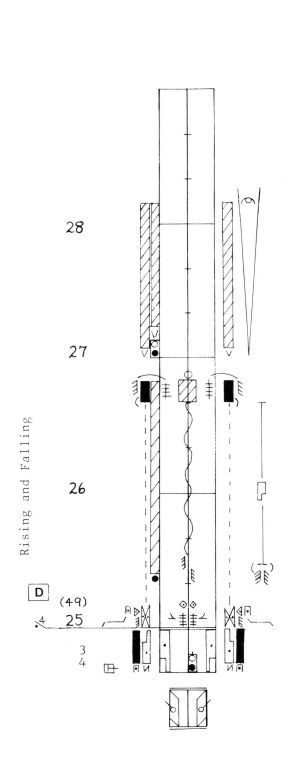

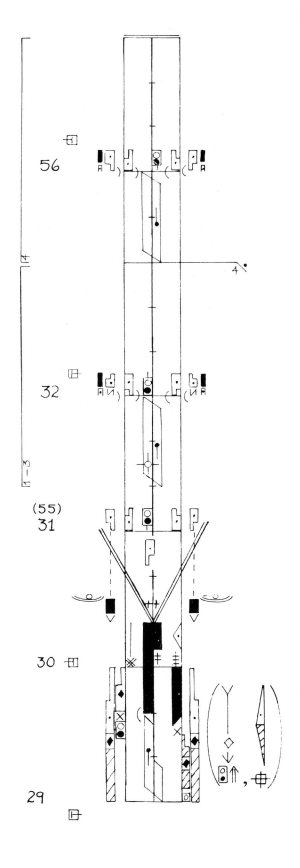

XI. SERIES OF SUCCESSIONS

83 Measures in Varying Meters

Each of these successions begins at the base, i.e. in the feet and progresses through the whole body, involving each part as it comes to it, and finally expends itself through the raised arms and hands. In XI A and B the succession is followed by a relaxation which starts with the fingertips and involves each part of the body bit by bit until the performer is once again in the original starting position.
It is important to achieve a complete succession through the whole body which, for these forward successions, starts from an extreme downward and backward position and progresses forward and upward from a push from the feet, on through the knees, pelvis and chest, and results in a taut arc. The base of the spine makes a sagittal circular path.

XI A. With Two Lifted Steps. 6 Measures of 6/8

Start in a 4th position foot-kneel, legs parallel, weight on the left knee, the right foot on the floor in front, body collapsed forward over the right knee. The sequence begins on count 3. To start the succession which goes right through the spine including the head, shift the weight to the right foot and bring the left to it both legs bent (counts 3, 4), at the same time raising the arms forward and up as the succession expends itself forward, bringing the performer to an extended, lifted position, high on the balls of both feet (counts 5, 6 and 1). From there take two high forward steps - right, left - on the notes in the music (counts 2 and 3), ending in a wide 4th position. Then relaxation takes over, starting in the arms led by the fingertips; as these lower, the head and torso become involved, moving down while lowering to the kneeling position, now on the right knee (counts 4, 5, 6 and 1). Hold count 2 before repeating. Perform this sequence a total of 3 times alternating sides.

XI B. With Sagittal Swing. 6 Measures of 6/8

The second variation in this series of successions begins and ends almost exactly like the first but with a different middle section. During the initial succession (counts 3, 4, 5, 6 and 1), only the left arm is raised, and only this arm is used for the energetic downward and backward swing during which the body lowers forward and rounded and the legs bend. This is immediately followed by a swing forward and upward to the high, lifted position (count 3) before the arm and body lower, sinking with a step forward on the right foot, and lowering to the kneeling position on the left knee (counts 4, 5, 6 and 1). Perform this sequence 3 times alternating sides; however, the third time end with normal standing, feet parallel, arms down.

With Two Lifted Steps

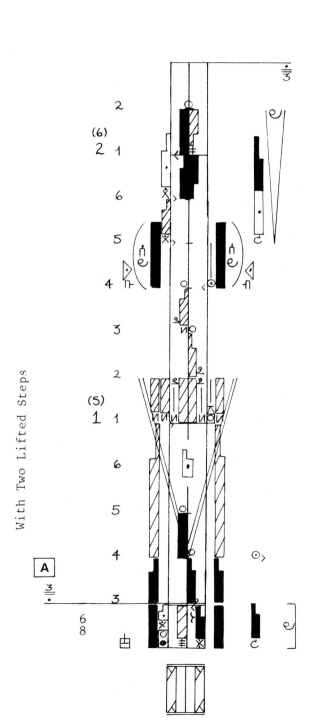

A

With Sagittal Swing

(transition)

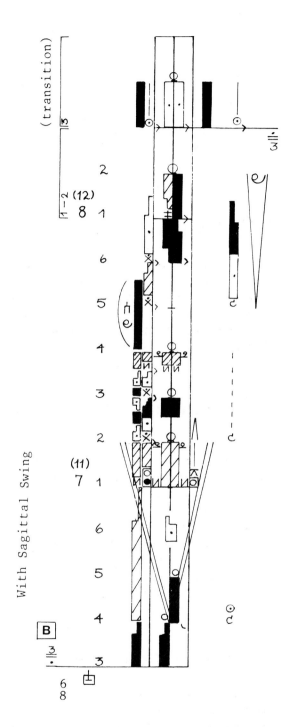

B

XI C. With a Prepatory Run and Swing. 4 Measures of 9/8

The third variation starts with three running steps forward - right, left, right - swinging the arms in natural opposition (counts 7, 8, 9), then with a spring onto both feet, sink with the torso forward as if you are going down into the floor (count 1). Push forward from the feet, bending the knees so that they almost touch the floor, then thrust the pelvis forward into the succession and follow through until you are again lifted on half-toe in a high arch (counts 2, 3, 4, 5 and 6). This time the arms move strongly forward, up and out, ending side horizontal as the upper body arches backward. This whole sequence is performed 4 times, alternating sides. At the end of the fourth time, there are three strong chords in the music during which (still on half-toe) the arms rise slowly and strongly to directly overhead (counts 7, 8 and 9).

XI D. With a Swinging Jump. 15 Measures of 3/4

Now a body and arm swing preparation combined with jumps lead into the body succession.

From the high lifted position, feet together, swing both arms strongly down and back with a force which on count 2 carries you off both feet into the air in a small jump, the torso forward horizontal, arms back (counts 1, 2, 3). Then swing the arms forward and lift again off the floor but still keeping the body low (counts 1, 2, 3). Next perform a body succession starting at the base of the spine and pushing through the balls of the feet; the knees and pelvis move forward and upward at the same time that the arms circle down, back and up in opposition to the circle of the hips (counts 1, 2, 3 and 1). These 4 measures are performed 4 times. On the final strong chord, collapse the whole torso forward from the hips.

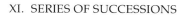

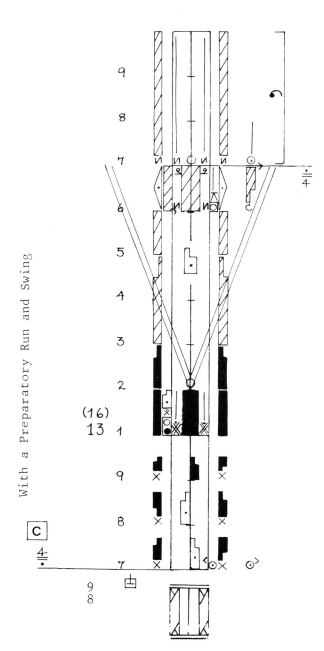

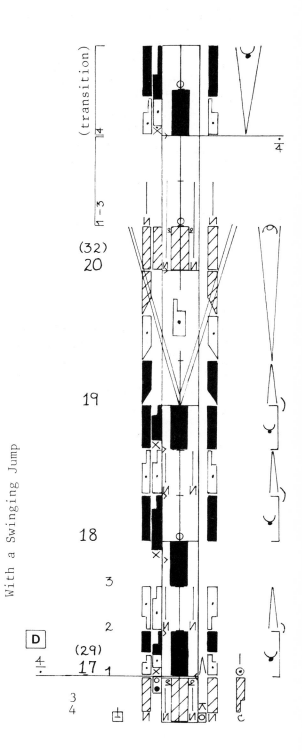

XI E. Accelerating Successions. 4 Measures of 4/4; 4 measures of 3/4; 2 measures of 4/4

Starting with the torso collapsed forward, arms down, feet together parallel, legs bent, the succession begins at the base of the spine. As the hips push forward and the succession moves through the whole spine to the head, release the right leg, lifting it forward from the floor, and rise on the left leg before allowing the weight to fall forward onto the right foot. The torso then drops forward, returning to the collapsed position. During this succession, the arms are completely relaxed, reacting passively to the movement. Repeat this phrase, alternating sides, 4 times. Then, when the meter changes to 3/4, perform 4 more times at a faster tempo, falling forward on count 2. A third increase in tempo (now again in 4/4) results in a smaller, but still complete movement performed as a walk, one succession occuring on each step, only the falling no longer occurs.

XI F. Succession with One Arm. 16 Measures of 3/4

Start facing stage right, legs comfortably turned out, arms relaxed at the sides. On the upbeat, the left arm begins a sagittal circle, backward and up; as the arm continues forward and down, the left foot points forward and the arm takes the torso forward with it; the supporting leg bends as the torso lowers. The arm concludes its forward sagittal circle with the hand touching the left foot (1 measure). During the forward succession which follows, initiation is from the hips and the left arm circles sagittally backward as the torso rises (1 measure). On count 3 of this measure, a catch step backward with the left foot leads into three forward walking steps - right, left, right (1 measure); the left arm, concluding its backward circle, ends down. Three more forward walking steps are taken in a small counterclockwise semi-circle to end facing stage left (4 measures altogether). This sequence is performed 4 times alternating sides. On the last time instead of circling, walk straight front, closing the feet on count 3.

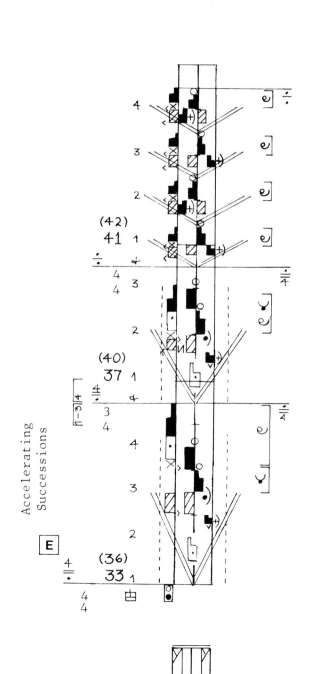

Accelerating Successions

E

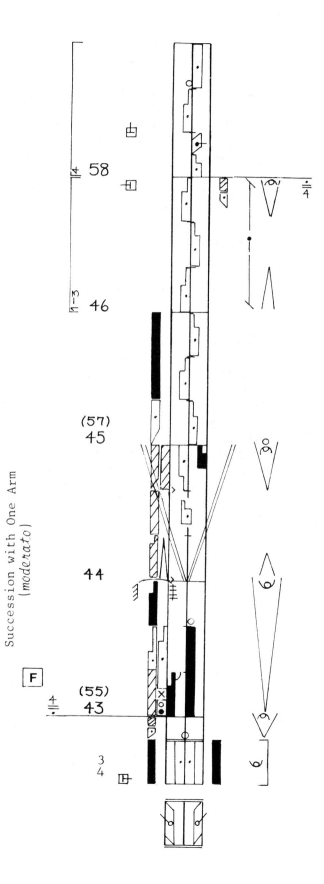

Succession with One Arm (*moderato*)

F

XI G. Circular Movement in Three Planes. 10 measures of slow 6/8

Start in 2nd position, legs comfortably turned out, with the left leg bent and thus more weight on the left foot, the torso inclined as far to the left as possible. The arms are down, relaxed; they have no special movements in this sequence, but are allowed to follow the torso movements passively. The first succession is in the lateral plane as the body pulls up and over to the right as though moving all the way from the left foot through to the right shoulder. After passing the vertical, the torso relaxes over to the right side as far as possible. Repeat the succession to the left (2 measures). Next the torso performs a horizontal circular path, extending from the left side to forward and on around to the right side. This path is then retraced, circling to the left (2 measures). The torso then moves to forward horizontal (1/4 circle, clockwise) and from there it returns to upright with a sequential movement progressing sagittally from the feet up through the pelvis and upper spine. Repeat these 5 measures.

XI H. Circular Movement in the Lateral Plane. 16 measures of 3/4

Start in 2nd position, weight over to the left in a deep lunge, the torso inclined as far as possible sideward to the left; the arms also to the left, following the line of the torso. A sideward sequential movement in the torso to the right carries the torso from left to right; the arms lag behind (i.e. over to the left) for as long as possible, then lower passively and, at the end of the sequential movement, return to 'overhead', i.e. to the right side in line with the torso (2 measures). Repeat this pattern alternating sides for a total of 4 times. After this, the music grows progressively faster, and as a result, during the next seven repeats of the pattern, the movements become spatially smaller until the body ends upright. The sequence concludes with a clap of the hands overhead, the feet closing sharply with a small spring on count 1 of the sixteenth measure.

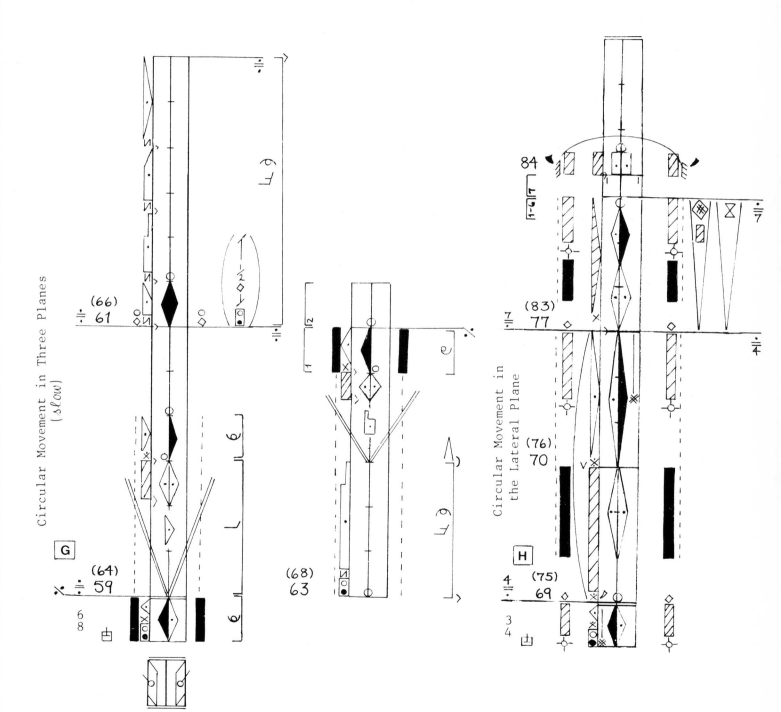

APPENDIX A
SHAWN'S ALPHABET OF BASIC STEPS

To my knowledge, Shawn was the first to establish an alphabet of basic steps for dance. By 'steps' Shawn means footwork specifically. One can see the origins of his alphabet quite clearly in the dance forms he encountered and used in his own choreography. Shawn's concern in making a study of the Alphabet was to include not only knowledge of the different steps, but also awareness of the importance of meticulous execution. To him a step was like a word in language – if it is not clearly enunciated, its meaning is not clear either.

For example, in the Polka, the 'hop–step–close–step is not a polka step if performed sloppily, as when a 'slide' is used instead of a 'close'. The reason for executing a 'step' and not a 'slide' is that originally the polka was a peasant step, danced on the grass or turf, i.e. not on a smooth, hard surface. Therefore the foot must be placed, rather than drawn, into place. Folk dances performed outdoors or on dirt floors usually avoid sliding because of the dust this would raise. Another example is the marked difference between a *posé* step (*piqué*) onto half toe and a rise (*relevé*) after the weight is already placed on that leg. Such differences in performance are small, but significant and meaningful. The student needs to be aware of all these differences.

In his method and approach to movement, Shawn believed that the dancer should be conscious of the *root* of the movement, just as a scholar knows the root meaning of the words he or she uses and thus can choose those which give the clearest expression to his or her thoughts. Once this basic understanding and clarity is established, the various 'steps' can be used in whatever variations wished. Without knowledge of correct movement, subsequent variations do not have the strength of a firm base. The five positions in ballet need to be clearly performed before one can use them freely. Shawn believed that every movement has meaning beyond just the execution. By teaching the Alphabet of Dance Steps with the names spoken as they were performed, Shawn demonstrated their importance and their differences.

Since Shawn's day, disciplines such as tap dance have evolved special names for various types of steps and foot movements. Terminology still varies somewhat and a few of the names Shawn used are no longer in use; I have presented Shawn's alphabet with revised explanations using present-day terminology.

Certain questions about the relevance of the selection in Shawn's alphabet are sure to arise. Would it have had more or less 'characters' if the English alphabet did not have 26 letters? There is no question that the list provides a useful guide for many types of dances, especially those which deal primarily with footwork; no doubt Shawn's conception made generations of students aware of the units of which so many dances are composed. Despite the changed terminology of dance, Shawn's alphabet is still of interest and value today.

Shawn composed the following simple sequence through which the Alphabet could be learned.

ALPHABET OF DANCE STEPS

1. STEP — A complete transference of weight from one foot to the other into a direction, the preparatory leg gesture moving clear of the floor.

2. CLOSE — Placing one foot next to the other, weight on both feet.

3. SLIDE — A directional transference of weight with the foot sliding along the floor.

4. DRAW — Sliding the foot into place, ending with it taking all the weight.

5. LEAP — A spring from one foot to the other.

6. HOP — A spring from one foot landing on the same foot.

7. JUMP — A spring from both feet landing on both feet.

8. EXTEND — Opening one leg out in the air without an emphasis on raising it.

9. CUT — A quick change of weight from one foot to the other in which one foot 'cuts' the weight out from under the other.

10. SWING — A curved movement downward and upward of the whole leg using gravity but without touching the floor.

11. BRUSH — A leg gesture (movement not taking weight) which slides briefly along the floor (may be similar to a 'swing').

12. BEAT — Also STAMP; a forceful taking of weight, usually in place.

13. TOUCH — The foot contacts the floor (usually in place, next to the other foot) without taking weight and without producing a sound.

14. KICK — A forceful, quick leg extension.

15. LUNGE — A long step onto a bent leg, the other foot remaining on the ground with a straight leg.

16. KNEEL — A lowering to one or both knees.

17. TWIST — A twist of the torso around its longitudinal axis.

18. TURN — A complete revolution of the body on one or both feet.

19. STANCE — A quick step on half-toe; *piqué* or *posé* in ballet (originally called a 'STROKE' by Shawn).

20. LIFT — A rise to half-toe from the whole (flat) foot.

21. RELEVE — A staccato rise through a slight lift of weight off the floor.

22. PLIE — A bending of the knee or knees.

23. CLAQUE — A beating together of the heels or soles of the feet in the air.

24. STOMP — An audible contact of the foot with the ground which does not take weight.

25. POINT — Placing the extended toe on the floor away from the supporting foot, the leg usually being straight.

26. TRANSFER — A shift of weight from one foot to both or *vice versa*.

APPENDIX A
ALPHABET OF BASIC STEPS

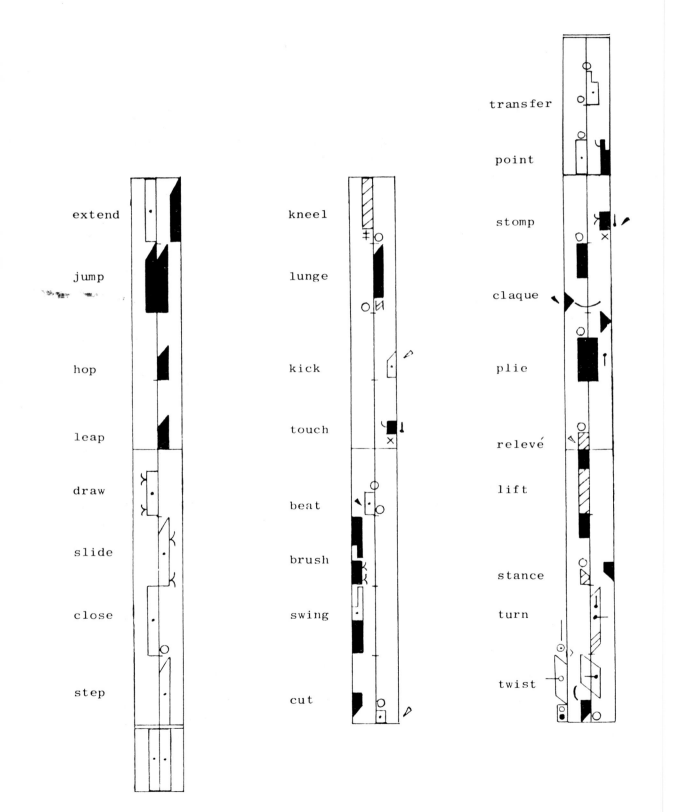

extend

jump

hop

leap

draw

slide

close

step

kneel

lunge

kick

touch

beat

brush

swing

cut

transfer

point

stomp

claque

plie

relevé

lift

stance

turn

twist

APPENDIX B

SHAWN BIOGRAPHY

Ted Shawn was born Edwin Myers Shawn in Kansas City, Missouri, in 1891, the son of an editor of the Kansas City Star. He grew up in Denver, Colorado and entered the university of Denver as a liberal arts student, but with preparation for the ministry in mind. Stricken with diphteria and, as a result partially paralysed for a year, his fight to regain mobility through body exercises led to an interest in dance and his decision to give up theological studies and to make dance his career. After a period of study with ballet teacher Hazel Wallack, he made his professional debut in Denver in 1911. Moving to Los Angeles he soon joined forces with Norma Gould, making one of the earliest motion pictures, *Dance of the Ages*. A 1913–14 coast-to-coast tour with a company of four dancers terminated in New York where he met Ruth St. Denis, became her partner, and soon after married her. Together in 1915 they founded Denishawn in Los Angeles, a school and performing company which was to have a most significant influence on the development of dance in America, nurturing the next generation of leaders of American modern dance, Martha Graham, Doris Humphrey, Charles Weidman and Jack Cole. Branches of Denishawn school sprouted and flourished in many cities. The company undertook tours of the U.S. and Canada, as well as an extended visit to the Orient in 1925–26.

In 1917 they produced the first service in a Christian church exclusively using dance as the medium of expression at the First Interdenominational Church in San Francisco. Shawn continued to present religious dances, not only in theatres but also for religious organizations. He was an early supporter of the Sacred Dance Guild.

Following the break up of Denishawn in 1932, Shawn turned to realizing an idea that was close to his heart, that of proving that dance was an activity suitable for men. With the formation of his men's group in 1933, he embarked on a seven-year campaign to establish in the minds of Americans the rightful place of men in dance, presenting a wide variety of choreographies for the group that made use of their vitality, strength and rhythmic sense. In 1940 the advent of the war saw the disbanding of the men dancers. Shawn took steps to establish what was soon to become the Jacob's Pillow Summer University of the Dance and the Jacob's Pillow Dance Festival. He built Jacob's Pillow into a dance center of international renown, presenting programs which sought to give equal opportunity to ballet, modern and ethnic forms. He presented newcomers as well as established stars and gave a first showing to new creations and experimental works. As impresario, he introduced to American audiences ten leading dancers of the Royal Danish Ballet (and subsequently other Royal Danish units), the National Ballet of Canada, the Celtic Ballet of Scotland, England's Ballet Rambert and other major companies and soloists.

Although continuing to dance into the 1960s, his public performances became less frequent and focussed on parts particularly suited to his maturity.

From the early days Shawn was deeply concerned with dance education. Being by build unsuited for ballet, he sought to create a dance technique built on fundamental movement principles. During the Denishawn period he established a teaching system which drew on the dance forms he encountered. He introduced the modern German dance to the students through Margarete Wallmann and introduced ethnic dance forms into American dance training.

As themes for his dances Shawn drew on American pioneers, the Spanish conquistador, American Indians, the American Negro, American folk dances, and on the contemporary American seaman, farmer, laborer, politician and artist. Ignoring traditional ballet music, he danced to Bach, Beethoven, Mozart, Honegger, Scriabin, Satie, and Vaughan Williams, as well as to music he had especially commissioned.

Shawn's belief in an educational program in dance centered on exposing students to both ballet and modern as well as various ethnic dance forms. This was achieved through personal contact in the dance technique classes, attending the weekly lecture series and, of course, seeing live performances in the theatre for which the weekly change in program provided a rich variety in content. It has been said that being at the Denishawn school and in the company was like a dance trip around the world. A comparable dance trip was provided by Shawn at Jacob's Pillow from the 1940s until his death. Students who were uncertain as to which form of dance best suited them had a unique opportunity to find out through the summer program that Shawn offered. The roster of names of those who have taught at Jacob's Pillow include famous performers and educationalists from across the U.S.A. as well as from abroad, and many ex-students have made their mark in the dance field.

Shawn was the first dancer in America to receive an honorary degree from an educational institution, this being Springfield College, in 1936. Subsequently he received many citations and honors including the Capezio Award, 1957, and the Dance Magazine Award in 1970. The most prestigious was the knighthood from King Frederick IX of Denmark who presented Shawn with the Cross of Dannebrog in 1958. The king broke a precedent of over 1000 years by giving a private audience to a foreigner other than an official Ambassador of State.

In 1987 the National Museum of Dance in Saratoga Springs, New York, honored Shawn as a founder of American dance by electing him to the nation's only Hall of Fame dedicated to Dance.

Shawn's philosophy of dance was both his educational credo and his theatrical aesthetic. In 1915 at the founding of Denishawn he encapsulated this when he wrote: "The art of the Dance is too big to be encompassed by any one system. On the contrary, the Dance includes all systems or schools of dance. Every way that any human being of any race or nationality, at any period of human history has moved rhythmically to express himself, belongs to the Dance. We endeavour to recognise and use all contributions of the past to the Dance and will continue to use all new contributions in the future."

Shawn died in January, 1972. The most visible memorial to him is the Ted Shawn Theatre at Jacob's Pillow, the first theatre built specifically for dance. But his ideas and ideals for dance live on through those who, directly or indirectly, were influenced by his universal view of dance and his belief in sound, fundamental principles in dance training.

SHAWN BIBLIOGRAPHY

Ruth St. Denis, Pioneer and Prophet, 1920
The American Ballet, 1926
Gods Who Dance, 1929
Fundamentals of the Dance Education, 1937
Dance We Must, 1940
How Beautiful Upon the Mountain, 1943
Every Little Movement: A Treatise on François Delsarte, 1954
16 Dances in 16 Rhythms, 1956
Thirty Three Years of American Dance, 1959
One Thousand and One Night Stands, 1960

For a complete bibliography of articles, photographs and dances choreographed see the Dictionary Catalog of the Dance Collection, Volume 9, New York Public Library.

MUSIC SCORE

I. General Stretching Set

II. Figure Eight Swings

III. Tension and Relaxation – Set One

IV. Tension and Relaxation – Set Two

V. Floor Set

VI. Three Jumps

VII. Walking – Running – Leaping

VIII. Long Adagio

IX. Single Arm Swing and Development

X. Three Delsarte Falls*

*Music for this exercise composed by Mary Campbell and is here printed with her permission.

Rising and Falling

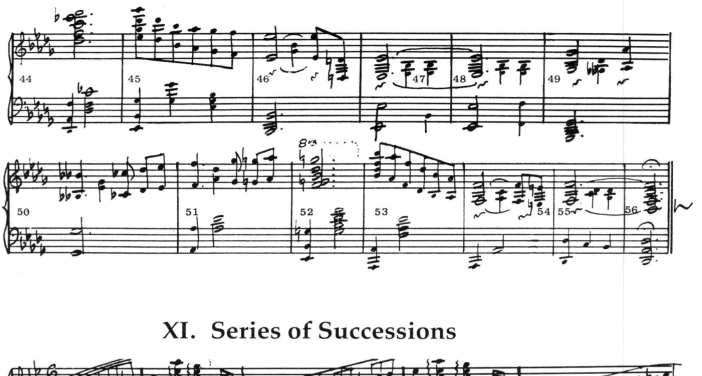

XI. Series of Successions

Alphabet

INDEX

The letter given after the page number, e.g. E, F, denotes the exercise on that page.